Literature in Perspective

General Editor: Kenneth H. Grose

George Bernard Shaw

Literature in Perspective

George Bernard Shaw

G. E. Brown

Evans Brothers Limited, London

Published by Evans Brothers Limited

Montague House, Russell Square, London, W.C.1

© G. E. Brown 1970

First published 1970

For Barbara and Patrick

Set in 11 on 12 point Bembo and printed in Great Britain by The Camelot Press Ltd., London and Southampton

237 44345 7 cased   PR 2417
237 44402 x limp

Literature in Perspective

Reading is a pleasure; reading great literature is a great pleasure, which can be enhanced by increased understanding, both of the actual words on the page and of the background to those words, supplied by a study of the author's life and circumstances. Criticism should try to foster understanding in both aspects.

Unfortunately for the intelligent layman and young reader alike, recent years have seen critics of literature (particularly academic ones) exploring slender ramifications of meaning, exposing successive levels of association and reference, and multiplying the types of ambiguity unto seventy times seven.

But a poet is 'a man speaking to men', and the critic should direct his efforts to explaining not only what the poet says, but also what sort of man the poet is. It is our belief that it is impossible to do the first without doing the second.

LITERATURE IN PERSPECTIVE, therefore, aims at giving a straightforward account of literature and of writers—straightforward both in content and in language. Critical jargon is as far as possible avoided; any terms that must be used are explained simply; and the constant preoccupation of the authors of the Series is to be lucid.

It is our hope that each book will be easily understood, that it will adequately describe its subject without pretentiousness so that the intelligent reader who wants to know about Donne or Keats or Shakespeare will find enough in it to bring him up to date on critical estimates.

Even those who are well read, we believe, can benefit from a lucid expression of what they may have taken for granted, and perhaps—dare it be said?—not fully understood.

K. H. G.

George Bernard Shaw

Bernard Shaw was one of the most prolific writers in English Literature, being the author of fifty-three plays, five novels, several volumes of literary and social essays, as well as countless thousands of words of journalism and letters. He was in addition possibly the most widely quoted figure of his day. His writing career spanned more than sixty years and it is as a playwright that he is chiefly remembered. I have not attempted to deal with all his plays, partly because of the limitations inevitably imposed in a book of this length, and partly because Shaw's shorter plays are mere squibs and it is arguable whether certain of the later plays can be called truly dramatic. I have tried to concentrate attention on the effectiveness of his plays as theatre while devoting one chapter (Chapter 7) to an examination of his non-dramatic prose writings. Chapters 2, 3 and 4—*The Early Plays, Shaw and Evolution* and *The Religious Plays*—deal chiefly with recurrent themes in Shaw's work, while Chapters 5 and 6—*Comedy* and *Characterisation*—are devoted primarily to an examination of techniques.

In the Reading List I have acknowledged those works which I have found most helpful in writing this book. *Collected Letters 1874–1897* edited by Dan. H. Laurence and *Theatrical Companion to Shaw* by Raymond Mander and Joe Mitchenson have proved invaluable.

The reference numbers of the quotations refer to pages in either *The Complete Plays* (CP) or *The Complete Prefaces* (CPBS).

I should like to thank Kenneth Grose for his helpful advice and unfailing encouragement at all stages in the production of this book.

G. E. B.

Contents

1. Biographical   *page* 9

2. The Early Plays   25

3. Shaw and Evolution   43

4. The Religious Plays   66

5. Comedy   93

6. Characterisation   121

7. The Prose Writings   139

    Reading List   157

    Index   159

The Author

G. E. Brown is Senior Lecturer in English at Avery Hill College of Education, Eltham, London.

Acknowledgements

The author and publishers are indebted to the following for permission to use illustrations: Bassano and Vandyk Studios for the cover photograph, the Birmingham Post and Mail Ltd., for the photograph of the Malvern Festival Group, the Raymond Mander and Joe Mitchenson Theatre Collection for the scene from *Heartbreak House*, and Central Press Photos Ltd., for the photograph of Shaw in old age.

They are also indebted to the Society of Authors, as agents for the Bernard Shaw Estate, for permission to quote from his works and to reproduce the engraving by Farleigh.

I

Biographical

The two best-known public figures in Britain in the first half of this century were Winston Churchill and Bernard Shaw. Both were controversial, and they both had the good fortune to live long lives, thereby having the maximum amount of time available to impress their views on the public. It is a well-known fact that the English warm towards famous old men who have earlier succeeded only in irritating them, and this was true in the case of Shaw. He deliberately built up a public image of himself as a vegetarian who wore Jaeger suits for health reasons, and who commented provocatively in the newspapers when asked for his opinion on matters of public interest. It was typical of him that when this campaign to keep Shaw in the limelight had succeeded overwhelmingly he should deny the truth of the picture. In 'A Warning from the Author', which prefaces *The Complete Plays of Bernard Shaw*, his readers are advised:

> . . . I must warn you, before you attempt to enjoy my plays, to clear out of your consciousness most resolutely everything you have ever read about me in a newspaper. Otherwise you will not enjoy them: you will read them with a sophisticated mind, and a store of beliefs concerning me which have not the slightest foundation either in prosaic fact or in poetic truth. In some unaccountable way I seem to cast a spell on journalists which makes them recklessly indifferent not only to common veracity, but to human possibility. The person they represent me to be not only does not exist but could not possibly exist.   CP v

This statement contains a core of truth, but an examination of a few of his published remarks will show that the journalists did not always invent to produce controversial news about Shaw.

Two incidents concerning the Shakespeare Memorial Theatre (as it then was) at Stratford are worth noting. In March 1926 the original Stratford theatre was burned down. Among the messages of condolence received from all over the world Shaw's voice rang out dissentingly: 'Stratford-upon-Avon is to be congratulated on the fire,' he told a reporter, going on to point out less startlingly that the town needed a modern theatre in which to play Shakespeare. When a new theatre was finally built it was opened by the Prince of Wales in April 1932. King George V left the opening ceremony in the hands of his son, preferring to go to the Cup Final himself. Shaw's secretary, Miss Blanche Patch, writes that: 'he accepted George the Fifth quite frankly as a lowbrow, and as such said he was quite right to go to a Cup Final instead of the inauguration of the Stratford Memorial Theatre, "one of the greatest events of his reign".'

Comments of this nature, together with his crisply stated views on subjects ranging from vegetarianism to Russian Communism, ensured that Shaw was seldom out of the public eye. He turned down high honours, including a peerage, during his lifetime, and by reason of longevity as much as anything else succeeded in gaining the affection of his adopted countrymen so that his death in 1950 caused many who were not theatre-goers or readers to mourn his passing. The fact that the fall that led to his death was caused while pruning an apple tree in his garden at the age of ninety-four must have drawn rueful admiration even from those who did not like his plays.

HIS EARLY LIFE

The determination to be known which Shaw showed so consistently can be partially explained by his origins and the subsequent insecurity of his early life. The best sources of information concerning these things are Shaw's own writings, although it should be borne in mind that Shaw is sometimes writing sixty or seventy years after the events he is describing, and he is, of necessity, subjective in his assessment of the situation. In many a preface, and particularly in a book published late in his career, *Sixteen Self Sketches*, he tells of the difficulties he faced as a youth, which were largely a result of the incompatibility of his father and mother. Shaw was born in Dublin in 1856. In the Preface to a volume of his music criticism, *London Music in 1888-9*, he wrote a memorable account of his mother:

> Technically speaking I should say she was the worst mother conceivable, always, however, within the limits of the fact that she was incapable of unkindness to any child, animal, or flower, or indeed to any person or thing whatsoever .... She went her own way with so complete a disregard and even unconsciousness of convention and scandal and prejudice that it was impossible to doubt her good faith and innocence; but it never occurred to her that other people, especially children, needed guidance or training, or that it mattered in the least what they ate and drank or what they did as long as they were not actively mischievous.   CPBS 853

This woman obviously needed to marry a strong-willed dependable man, but instead married George Carr Shaw. He was an unsuccessful wholesaler in the corn trade, and, according to his son:

> ... in principle an ardent teetotaller .... Unfortunately his conviction in this matter was founded on personal experience. He was the victim of a drink neurosis which cropped up in his family from time to time: a miserable affliction, quite unconvivial, and accompanied by torments of remorse and shame.
>
> Preface, LONDON MUSIC IN 1888-9   CPBS 854

Shaw's mother was unaware of her husband's weakness when she married him, although she discovered empty bottles in a cupboard during her honeymoon and attempted to leave him. However, her relatives had disowned her, as a result of the marriage, so she stayed with her husband. The marriage was not successful, and Shaw's father's business slowly deteriorated. The three children of the marriage were brought up by neglectful servants, and Shaw writes of 'the little Shaw household where a thoroughly disgusted and disillusioned woman was suffering from a hopelessly disappointing husband and three uninteresting children grown too old to be petted like the animals and birds she was so fond of, to say nothing of the humiliating inadequacy of my father's income' (CPBS 858).

It is possible that Bernard Shaw would have remained in Ireland working as a clerk, as he did in his first job, if it had not been for his mother's interest in music. She had a good mezzo-soprano voice and took lessons from George John Vandaleur Lee, an unorthodox teacher who had discovered a new method of teaching singing. Lee was a great organiser of concerts and operas, and used Mrs. Shaw as 'not only prima donna and chorus leader but general musical factotum in the whirlpool of ... activity' (CPBS 855). The Shaws and Lee set up house together, and although Lee supplanted Mr. Shaw as the effective head of the household, Bernard Shaw records that there was no unpleasantness or friction between the two men.

After some years Lee went to London, having decided that Dublin fame was not enough for him. He was soon fashionable as a teacher, but Shaw records that he became something of a charlatan in order to pay the rent. Mrs. Shaw decided to follow Lee to London and set up herself as a teacher of singing, imparting Lee's unique method (shades of Eliza Doolittle's scheme to combat Higgins here), and she hoped that her elder daughter would succeed as an opera singer. Mrs. Shaw did not have immediate success in her ambitions for her daughter and herself, but later became a much sought after teacher of music in schools.

Bernard Shaw and his father had been left behind in Dublin, where the son worked as cashier to a firm of land agents. He was much more interested in painting, music and philosophical discussion than in business, but his quick-wittedness ensured rapid promotion to responsibility in the firm. However, he feared that to stay in Dublin would prevent him from achieving his literary ambitions, and so, in March 1876, he gave notice and followed his mother and sister to London.

EARLY YEARS IN LONDON

Shaw had not received anything like a systematic education in Dublin. He had been taught by a governess at home when he was very young, and afterwards he had attended the Wesleyan Connexional School and two or three more schools. He later claimed to have learned little from formal instruction, and it is no doubt true that he was largely self-taught. He has recorded how he read Dickens, Defoe and Shakespeare, and how the Dublin National Gallery and the music heard in his own home meant more to him than any lessons. When he arrived in London he determined to further his education, and set about learning to sing under his mother's guidance. He had no intention of beginning regular work, but had to go through the motions of obtaining employment, sometimes even succeeding. He worked for a while for the Edison Telephone Company, but spent most of his time writing articles for newspapers (which were invariably rejected) and he completed five novels in the period 1879–83.

In nine years Shaw earned only £6 from his writing, yet we should note that he *completed* his five novels. There was nothing frivolous in his application to literature, and it was natural in an age dominated by the novel that he should see himself as a novelist long before he turned to writing for the theatre. Day after day Shaw would go to the Reading Room of the British Museum to further his education and to write. His mother supported him during this period, and there is no doubt an echo of Shaw's feelings when he was an unsuccessful writer in Tanner's speech in Act One of *Man and Superman*, written in 1903:

> The true artist will let his wife starve, his children go barefoot, his mother drudge for his living at seventy, sooner than work at anything but his art. CP 341

It was in 1882, in the Reading Room of the British Museum, that Shaw first read Karl Marx, whose writings were to have such a great influence on him. From that point on Shaw was a socialist, eager to reform English society. On 5 September 1884 he joined the Fabian Society, whose members included H. G. Wells and Sidney Webb, the economist. Sidney Webb and his wife, Beatrice, were later to found the London School of Economics and the *New Statesman*, the socialist weekly magazine. Shaw took every opportunity that offered itself of speaking in debates on political and social questions, often attending meetings on three evenings a week. He would never accept a fee for speaking. These meetings gave him immense confidence, and it is likely that the debating influenced the style of his plays when he came to write them. So many of them are debate-dramas, and the experience he had gained in arguing a case must have helped in their construction, just as the five rejected novels had helped to form style and fluency long before Shaw became famous as a playwright.

The years in the Reading Room of the British Museum were not only profitable in terms of learning. It was there, in 1883, that Shaw met William Archer, the Scottish dramatic critic, who is now remembered chiefly as the first translator of Ibsen's plays into English. Archer was the dramatic critic of *The World*, and he was able to obtain some book-reviewing for Shaw on *The Pall Mall Gazette*. This was Shaw's first regular employment as a writer, and early in 1886 Archer, who was also acting as art critic of *The World*, in spite of a self-confessed lack of knowledge about painting, was instrumental in Shaw's taking over the job. In his first year of journalism Shaw earned £112.

Archer did not only help Shaw to gain a footing as a journalist. He introduced him to Ibsen's plays and encouraged him to begin work on a play that they were to write in collaboration. What eventually saw the light of day as *Widowers' Houses*, Shaw's first play, began under the working title of *Rheingold*, the plot having been suggested by Archer in 1884. Shaw was to write the dialogue. In October 1887 Shaw read the first two acts of the play to Archer. They did not please him and he withdrew from the collaboration. Shaw put the play aside, only taking it up again in 1892. The failure of the writing partnership did not destroy the great regard that the two men had for each other, and Shaw's interest in social drama can be traced largely to the influence of Ibsen in Archer's translations.

Before Shaw was to make a name for himself as a playwright he was to spend several more years as a critic. Archer had seen him started as a book reviewer and art critic. Between 1888 and 1894 Shaw was a very down-to-earth music critic, first on *The Star* and then on *The World*. His brief was to be intelligent without being esoteric. Anyone who looks at his music criticism, written under the name of Corno di Bassetto, will realise how well he succeeded. He had the ability to describe a performance so that the reader feels as though he were there, and the musical comment is constantly enlivened by a sardonic wit:

Miss Osmond, who appeared at Steinway Hall on the 16th, is a young English pianist who has studied in England from first to last, which is at present, I am sorry to say, a course rather patriotic than wise. *The World* 24 February 1892

I earnestly advise the young ladies of England, whether enrolled in the Guild of St. George or not, to cultivate music solely for the love and need of it, and to do it in all humility of spirit, never forgetting that they are most likely inflicting all-but-unbearable annoyance on every musician within earshot, instead of rendering 'assistance to others'. The greatest assistance the average young-lady musician can render to others is to stop. *The World* 2 May 1894

At the end of 1894 Shaw became dramatic critic of the *Saturday Review*, which was edited by the extraordinary Frank Harris, perhaps better known today as a writer of pornography. Shaw's dramatic criticism is among the most brilliant ever produced, and there can be no doubt that his work in the theatre in this vein helped him later as a playwright. He was not, however, directly stimulated towards dramatic authorship by his new profession. We have noted how he began thinking about *Widowers' Houses* as early as 1884, and by the time he began to write for the *Saturday Review* he had already written several plays which had been performed, including *Arms and the Man*. He explained his position in a letter to Archer, dated 28 December 1894:

It is questionable whether it is quite decent for a dramatic author to be also a dramatic critic; but my extreme reluctance to make myself dependent for my bread and butter on the acceptance of my plays by managers tempts me to hold to the position that my real profession is that by which I can earn my bread in security. Anyhow, I am prepared to do anything which will enable me to keep my plays for twenty years with perfect tranquillity if it takes that time to educate the public into wanting them.

Although he was now a playwright whose plays were being produced, it was many years before he was able to rely on theatrical success in England. *Arms and the Man* was acted on fifty occasions at the Avenue Theatre in 1894, but other early plays were lucky to achieve a dozen performances. In fact, Shaw made more money from foreign rights in his first years in the theatre than he did from royalties on productions in England. The relative lack of success of his plays on the stage also caused him to do as Ibsen had done before him. He took great care to see that his plays were brought out in attractive reading editions, with very full stage directions, so that the person reading a play at home was given the greatest possible help in imagining an ideal performance. Many actors and critics have felt since that the stage directions, which are often the length of short essays, act as a stranglehold on the reader or performer, but there is no doubt that they make a play easier to read than if it were left with bare, technical directions only. It must be admitted, however, that some of Shaw's introductory comments are more suited to a novel than a play, and would be impossible for an actor to convey to an audience. For instance, when Sir Colenso Ridgeon is described in Act One of *The Doctor's Dilemma*, we are told that 'in figure and manner he is more the young man than the titled physician. Even the lines in his face are those of overwork and restless scepticism, perhaps partly of curiosity and appetite, rather than that of age' (CP 505).

In his lifetime Shaw was lucky in forming alliances with distinguished, sympathetic men of the theatre, and, in spite of the running battle he had with Sir Henry Irving, whose style of acting he believed often subjugated a play to the actor's personality, he thought highly of good actors. When he died a large proportion of his money was left to the Royal Academy of Dramatic Act, the major drama school in London. His connections with two managements were vital to his theatrical development.

In 1904 Harley Granville Barker, at that time a leading actor and producer, although perhaps better remembered today as a playwright and leading critic of the plays of Shakespeare, began working at the Royal Court Theatre, London. In partnership with J. E. Vedrenne, Barker produced eleven of Shaw's plays during the years 1904 to 1907. Among the plays produced at the Royal Court were *Man and Superman*, in which Barker played the leading part of Tanner in a make-up which deliberately resembled Shaw, and *Major Barbara*, which numbered the Prime Minister, Balfour, among its audience when it was first performed in 1905.

Shaw was by this time gaining the recognition of the type of audience that he wanted to attract to the theatre; humane, intelligent people who were ready to listen to his socialist message. He had married an Irish millionairess, Charlotte Payne-Townshend, in 1898, and, as a consequence of her financial support, had been able to leave dramatic criticism. The Vedrenne–Barker management gave him the beginnings of true financial independence, but in 1907 the partnership began to break up when Barker took over the Savoy Theatre and left the Royal Court. The new venture was not successful.

By the time Shaw met his next theatrical godfather a World War had taken place, and he was one of the most successful dramatists writing. In 1923 he was approached by the Birmingham millionaire, Barry Jackson, who had founded the Birmingham Repertory Theatre in 1913. Jackson had already included several of Shaw's plays in his seasons at the theatre, and he asked permission to stage the first British production of *Back to Methuselah*. The play is in five parts, and when first produced required four evenings and a matinée to be performed. Shaw is reputed to have asked Barry Jackson if his wife and family were provided for, and to have received the answer that he was a bachelor. From this time onwards Shaw was to be closely associated with Jackson, who presented several of his plays in London, and particularly at the Malvern Festival, which was founded in 1929.

Between the writing of *Saint Joan* (1923) and *The Apple Cart* (1929) Shaw produced no new plays. In 1928 he published the first edition of what is now known as *The Intelligent Woman's Guide to Socialism, Capitalism, Sovietism and Fascism*, which took three years to write. In 1929 he returned to the theatre. Barry Jackson, who lived at Malvern, decided to present a short summer festival there. The first season was devoted entirely to Shaw's plays, and the climax was the first English production of *The Apple Cart*. The festival continued annually under Barry Jackson's management until 1938, when the direction was taken over by Roy Limbert. Among Shaw's plays which received their first performances at Malvern were *Too True to be Good*, in 1932, *The Simpleton of the Unexpected Isles*, in 1935, and Shaw's last worthwhile, full-length play, *In Good King Charles's Golden Days*, which was presented in 1939.

THE OLD MAN

The Apple Cart is the last play by Shaw that can be expected to retain its place on the stage as a major product of its author. Yet Shaw continued to write plays up until the year of his death, 1950. In 1947, in the Preface to *Buoyant Billions*, he writes movingly of the aged writer's problems:

> I commit this to print within a few weeks of completing my 92nd year. At such an age I should apologize for perpetrating another play or presuming to pontificate in any fashion. I can hardly walk through my garden without a tumble or two; and it seems out of all reason to believe that a man who cannot do a simple thing like that can practise the craft of Shakespear. Is it not a serious sign of dotage to talk about oneself, which is precisely what I am now doing? Should it not warn me that my bolt is shot, and my place silent in the chimney corner?
>
> Well, I grant all this; yet I cannot hold my tongue nor my pen. As long as I live I must write. If I stopped writing I should die for wanting of something to do.   CPBS 891

He had outlived all his friends, and his wife had died in 1943. In July 1950 the Arts Theatre Club put on a special production of *Heartbreak House* in honour of his ninety-fourth birthday, but Shaw was by this time far too old and frail to go to the theatre.

In his later years he was apt to refuse permission for his plays to be performed, as he suffered from the delusion that the Inland Revenue would cause him to pay out more in tax than the productions would earn.

After he died in 1950 Shaw's reputation suffered the decline that is common to most writers in the years immediately following their death. Gradually, however, his plays have returned to prominence, and there can be no doubt that his ability to write parts that appeal to actors will ensure his survival in the theatre, even though vast plays, such as the full version of *Man and Superman*, and *Back to Methuselah*, are unlikely to be played more than once in a generation.

WHAT KIND OF WRITER?

In the individual analyses which follow in later chapters I have tried to show how Shaw's plays work dramatically. A few general remarks may prove helpful at this point.

Shaw began writing for the theatre when he realised that his social viewpoint could be disseminated most widely through drama. He was greatly influenced in this direction by the social plays of Ibsen. It is important to note that though what he had to say was revolutionary in the English theatre, he was not, at first, a great innovator in form.

As a boy in Dublin Shaw had attended many performances by such actors as Barry Sullivan, and we have seen how he later came to work in the theatre as a critic. It is not surprising to find that he took over many of the familiar devices of Victorian drama, and made use of them in his plays. In a conversation with his biographer, Hesketh Pearson, Shaw once said, 'Shavian plots are as silly as Shakespearean plots, and, like Shakespeare's, they are all stolen from other writers'. It is true that in plays such as *Mrs. Warren's Profession*, *The Devil's Disciple* and *Arms and the Man* Shaw introduces such characters as the fallen woman and the supremely heroic soldier, and situations such as the last-minute rescue of Dick Dudgeon from the gallows. These would all be familiar theatrical currency to the playgoers of the time, but, as we shall see in later chapters, Shaw brought his own individual touch to the way in which the characters and situations were used. Generally he took a familiar theatrical type or situation and reversed it, so that his audience was forced to reassess things radically. Paradox became Shaw's chief weapon, but the fact remains that the form of Shaw's early plays was not revolutionary.

As he became firmly established as a dramatist he felt able to allow his own interests to prevail, sometimes at the expense of theatrical effectiveness. His later works, such as *The Apple Cart*, and *The Simpleton of the Unexpected Isles*, are often platform discussions rather than plays. It is easy to see the way things were going, even in plays widely accepted as theatrical successes, such as *Saint Joan*. Nevertheless, it is difficult to blame too severely the dramatist who turned the attention of the theatrical world away from the self-centred actor-managers who were in charge when Shaw began to write, and directed it towards the author.

The variety of Shaw's plays is something that is sometimes overlooked. He was temperamentally not fitted for writing in the tragic manner, and many readers find him at his weakest when he attempts to be 'poetic', as at the death of Dubedat in *The Doctor's Dilemma* and in some of Joan's speeches in the trial scene in *Saint Joan*. His strengths are dealt with in the chapters that follow. However, it may be interesting to note here that he was the author of some twenty one-act plays, as well as those of conventional theatrical length, and I have already mentioned the five parts of *Back to Methuselah*, perhaps the longest play ever written.

With the coming of the 'talkies' to the cinema it was inevitable that Shaw would be asked for permission to film his plays. After showing initial reluctance he agreed, on condition that he retained complete control over the scripts. During his lifetime he would not allow any cutting of his plays on the stage or on radio, and he stuck to the same principle when it came to dealing with film producers. He failed to realise that a good film can often make a point visually in seconds which would take minutes of dialogue to communicate. For the films of *Pygmalion* (1938), *Major Barbara* (1940-1) and *Caesar and Cleopatra* (1945) Shaw was even persuaded to write additional scenes and dialogue. To the end of his life he was anxious to communicate his message to the largest possible audience, and the cinema offered the means of doing this.

THE WORK

Shaw is remembered chiefly as a playwright, and it is on his dramatic writing that comment has been concentrated in this book. His career as a successful dramatist spanned almost sixty years. He lived through the Boer War and two World Wars, and his lifetime was perhaps the greatest period of social change that Europe has ever known. When he began to write, poverty was the greatest evil facing him; by the end of his life the Welfare State had been established, women had gained the vote and higher education was available for all who qualified for it. Many of the abuses that had disappeared had done so because of the changed climate of opinion that Shaw's plays helped to create.

In the *Theatrical Companion to Shaw*, published in London in 1954, Raymond Mander and Joe Mitchenson list Shaw's plays with their dates of composition. The plays are as follows:

Widowers' Houses	1885–1892
The Philanderer	1893
Mrs. Warren's Profession	1893–1894
Arms and the Man	1894
Candida	1894–1895
The Man of Destiny	1895
You Never Can Tell	1895–1896
The Devil's Disciple	1896–1897
Caesar and Cleopatra	1898
Captain Brassbound's Conversion	1899
The Admirable Bashville	1901
Man and Superman	1901–1903
John Bull's Other Island	1904
How He Lied to Her Husband	1904
Major Barbara	1905
Passion, Poison, and Petrifaction	1905

The Doctor's Dilemma	1906
The Interlude at the Playhouse	1907
Getting Married	1908
The Shewing-up of Blanco Posnet	1909
Press Cuttings	1909
The Fascinating Foundling	1909
The Glimpse of Reality	1909
Misalliance	1909–1910
The Dark Lady of the Sonnets	1910
Fanny's First Play	1911
Androcles and the Lion	1912
Overruled	1912
Pygmalion	1912–1913
Great Catherine	1913
The Music-Cure	1913
O'Flaherty, V.C.	1915
The Inca of Perusalem	1916
Augustus Does His Bit	1916
Annajanska, the Wild Grand Duchess	1917
Heartbreak House	1913–1919
Back to Methuselah	1918–1920
Jitta's Atonement	1922
Saint Joan	1923
The Apple Cart	1929
Too True to be Good	1931
Village Wooing	1933
On The Rocks	1933
The Simpleton of the Unexpected Isles	1934
The Six of Calais	1934
The Millionairess	1935
Cymbeline Refinished	1937
Geneva	1938
In Good King Charles's Golden Days	1939
Buoyant Billions	1946–1948
Shakes versus Shav	1949
Farfetched Fables	1949–1950
Why She Would Not	1950

Jitta's Atonement is an adaptation of an Austrian play by Sieg-fried Trebitsch, who translated many of Shaw's plays into German. *Why She Would Not* was unpublished at the time of Shaw's death, and has never been performed. The typescript is in the British Museum.

It is obviously impossible to comment on all of the plays in a book of this length. Some readers will inevitably find that their particular favourite is merely mentioned or perhaps even omitted from discussion. It is hoped, however, that the com-mentaries which follow will provide clues towards the way in which a Shaw play should be read. I have tried to keep in mind at all times that the plays are meant to be performed. Ideally one should see a play by Shaw acted before reading it. This is not always possible, but I hope that a reader of this book will find some help in constructing an ideal performance of a play in his imagination.

SPELLING

Shaw took great care to see that his plays were printed exactly as he intended. In some ways he was idiosyncratic about this. Three points to look out for when reading his work are:

1. He usually omitted apostrophes in contractions. 'Cannot' becomes 'cant' in Shaw, not 'can't'. 'Will not' becomes 'wont', not 'won't'.

2. When he wished to emphasise a word Shaw did not use italics. He lengthened the spaces between the letters of the word to be emphasised, and sometimes the difference in spacing is difficult to spot, especially if one is reading quickly.

   Here are two examples:

   Oh, you coward, you havnt danced with m e for years.

   Is t h a t the way you feel towards us?

'Me' and 'that' are the words that Shaw is stressing in these sentences from *Androcles and the Lion* Prologue (CP 686) and *Pygmalion* Act Four (CP 741).

3. Sometimes Shaw's spelling appears unusual. He was in the habit of writing 'shew' instead of the more conventional 'show', and he dropped redundant vowels in certain words. He wrote 'humor', 'honor' and 'color' instead of 'humour', 'honour' and 'colour'. There are many more examples, most of which do not bother the reader after he has met them a few times.

2

The Early Plays

'PLAYS UNPLEASANT'

Throughout his life Shaw was passionately interested in questions of social reform and the remedying of evils caused by poverty. As we have seen, he was a brilliant speaker for the Fabian Society and also became a vestryman (or local councillor) for the St. Pancras area of London, but he saw that the way for him to bring unpleasant facts about social conditions before the widest possible audience was to use the theatre as his platform. Certain of his more popular plays, such as *Pygmalion*, are, if we read them with attention, extremely critical of a society that can condemn its poorer members to a life of drudgery and insecurity while they remain in health, and can send them to the workhouse when they become sick and old. But *Pygmalion* and *The Millionairess*, which contain a great deal of social criticism, are too successful in other ways for the message they carry to make its greatest effect; we remember them for their wit and humour and startling situations rather than for their condemnation of sweated labour.

However, in the three plays contained in the volume of *Plays Unpleasant*, first published in 1898, Shaw deals with social problems in a way that leaves his audience, or readers, unable to escape the moral that he himself points in his Preface. Here he states: 'I must, however, warn my readers that my attacks are directed against themselves, not against my stage figures' (CPBS 727). He insists that the evils of slum landlordism, prostitution and the subjection of women to men under antiquated marriage laws are the responsibility of everybody who fails to take his public duties as a citizen seriously; if his readers realise that such evils exist and do nothing to try to remedy the situation they are, in Shaw's view, as guilty as the people who profit by the exploitation of those weaker than themselves. This is not a doctrine calculated to comfort, and it is not surprising that the plays in *Plays Unpleasant* have never attained great popularity in the theatre, although, as we shall see, this can be partially accounted for by the censorship system which prevented public performances of *Mrs. Warren's Profession* in this country until 1925, over thirty years after the play was written.

In the prefaces to the plays contained in this volume Shaw tells us all we need to know about how the three plays came to be written, and incidentally gives an account of his amusing yet infuriating experiences in trying to get a licence for *Mrs. Warren's Profession* to be publicly performed. We learn that *Widowers' Houses*, Shaw's first play, was begun in 1885 in collaboration with William Archer, the dramatic critic and translator of Ibsen into English. Archer supplied the outline of the play and Shaw was to provide the dialogue. Shaw writes: 'Laying violent hands on his thoroughly planned scheme for a sympathetically romantic "well made play" of the Parisian type then in vogue, I perversely distorted it into a grotesquely realistic exposure of slum landlordism, municipal jobbery, and the pecuniary and matrimonial ties between them and the pleasant people with "independent" incomes who imagine that such sordid matters do not touch their own lives' (CPBS 719). Not surprisingly Archer was irritated by Shaw's changes of emphasis and withdrew from the collaboration. The play was put on one side until 1892 when Shaw completed it 'and handed it over to Mr. Grein, who launched it at the public in the Royalty Theatre with all its original tomfooleries on its head. It made a sensation out of all proportion to its merits or even its demerits; and I at once became infamous as a playwright' (CPBS 719).

The Mr. Grein mentioned in Shaw's preface was at that time promoting a venture known as the Independent Theatre, which was formed to bring drama dealing with problems of the day before an intelligent public. The plays of Ibsen were performed by Grein's company, but unfortunately plays of real merit by English authors were hard to find. We can compare the situation at the time with that which existed at London's Royal Court Theatre a few years ago, where, apart from the plays of John Osborne, almost all the productions lost a great deal of money.

In 1893 Shaw wrote another play, *The Philanderer*, in which he deals with the subject of marriage and its limitations, particularly for women. The play is not tremendously successful, although it contained occasional shafts of Shavian wit aimed at targets which were to be returned to later, such as the medical profession. Nevertheless *The Philanderer* moves at quite a pace and contains several good acting parts. Grein's company at that time was not capable of the highly-polished comic acting that the play needed and so for a second time Shaw laid a play aside unperformed; it was not in fact produced publicly until 1907.

Once again Shaw tried to oblige the Independent Theatre with a play and he wrote for them *Mrs. Warren's Profession*, only to have its production blocked by the officials of the Lord Chamberlain's department. The frank treatment of prostitution and the fact that the play contains a reference to a relationship which might turn out to be incestuous proved too much for the censors to accept in the 1890s. The idea of a production was abandoned and the play had to wait until 1925 for its first professional performance.

These three plays have never been performed as frequently as many of Shaw's other plays. It is interesting to note, however, that within a period of eight months in 1965 and 1966 they between them achieved five professional productions of merit; three in London, one in Bristol and one in Manchester. The critical reaction was in general one of mild surprise that the plays should revive so well. Why, in fact, do they excite our interest?

I think it is because Shaw has in each play taken a strong central situation and surrounded it, or decorated it, with the superficial trimmings which attract the casual theatre-goer. He never allows his concern with his message to turn him into a preacher as he does in some of his later plays. He shows a certainty of touch in his contrivance of amusing situations and characters in *The Philanderer*, for instance, that many a writer ambitious only to entertain would envy, and one is often aware while reading the plays of a verbal wit that makes use of epigram and paradox in a way that recalls Wilde, who in fact did not write his comedies until a few years after these plays of Shaw's were written. In addition, Shaw realised the necessity for the introduction of recognisable comic types. In *Mrs. Warren's Profession* and *Widowers' Houses* we have Cokane and Frank Gardner, the one a cultivated snob, the other a young man who takes pride in his inability to be serious about anything, and these characters are skilfully manipulated by the author to gain the amused attention of the audience, although in the case of Frank with his mannered repartee we today perhaps find him as irritating as Vivie Warren finally does. It is obvious, however, when we examine the plays, or better still experience them in the theatre, that Shaw had from the first an uncommon gift for knowing what would capture the attention of an audience. Once he had done this he was able to devote his skill to putting over his message.

Most people would agree, I think, that, in spite of Shaw's amusing self-portrait in the character of Charteris, *The Philanderer* is the least satisfying of the three plays. There is much to admire in the other two plays in the way of wit and characterisation, but finally we remember *Widowers' Houses* and *Mrs. Warren's Profession* for two or three scenes of almost overwhelming power in which Shaw allows his characters to state his case that a society based solely on the profit motive is a corrupt society. The solid core of each play is a discussion scene in which debate is raised to the level of high drama by the force of truth and the excellence of Shaw's rhetoric. The scene in which Sartorius explains to Trench (who is revolted to hear that his prospective father-in-law is a slum landlord) that he himself profits by the system, as his income is derived from a mortgage on property owned by Sartorius, is remarkable for its forcefulness and lack of cant. Even today the scene has relevance. Shaw permits us to see that Sartorius is not a tyrant, but is himself a victim of the wretched system when, later in the play, we are told that his mother was an exploited washerwoman. It would have been remarkable indeed if Sartorius had not developed the attitude he shows in the play towards money and the poor after such an upbringing.

The central figure of *Mrs. Warren's Profession* is Vivie Warren, a twentytwo-year-old Cambridge graduate in mathematics. She intends to set up chambers in the City and put her knowledge at the disposal of the business world. The impression we get of her in the early sections of the play is of a self-confident, unsentimental, even hard, young woman. She is a typical 'New Woman', cast in the mould of Beatrice Potter, the economist who married Shaw's friend, Sidney Webb, and the character obviously exerted a great deal of influence over many young women at the time of the play's first production in 1902, as can be seen from a reading of H. G. Wells's novel *Ann Veronica* (1909). In Chapter Five Ann Veronica is looking for work, having run away from home:

> Her ideas of women's employment and a modern woman's pose in life were based largely on the figure of Vivie Warren in *Mrs. Warren's Profession*. She had seen *Mrs. Warren's Profession* furtively with Hetty Widgett from the gallery of a Stage Society performance one Monday afternoon. Most of it had been incomprehensible to her, or comprehensible in a way that checked further curiosity, but the figure of Vivien, hard, capable, successful, and bullying, and ordering about a veritable Teddy in the person of Frank Gardner, appealed to her.

The action of most of the play takes place in and around a country cottage in Surrey, where Vivie is visited by her mother, who spends most of her time abroad, and two of her mother's friends, Sir George Crofts and Mr. Praed. It is evident from an early conversation between Vivie and Praed that there is something of a mystery about Mrs. Warren, and it is upon this that the play hinges. Gradually we learn that Mrs. Warren's life is not 'respectable' and that there is some doubt as to the identity of Vivie's father. Two more characters are introduced in the first act, Frank Gardner, a gay young man who is in love with Vivie, and his rather foolish father, the local vicar. The act ends on a note of high drama when the Reverend Samuel Gardner recognises Mrs. Warren as a figure from his wild past.

As the play progresses it becomes more complicated. Mrs.

Warren shows a great concern for the future of her daughter, whom she wishes to protect from Frank's advances, particularly when she learns that he will bring no money with him if he marries. Hints are dropped that point to the possibility of Frank and Vivie being half-brother and sister—it was this relationship that was one of the reasons for the play being banned when it was first written—and we learn that Crofts is interested in Vivie, to the great annoyance of her mother who knows what a reprobate he is. Act Two ends with the brilliant scene in which Vivie confronts her mother with a demand for information about her father and her relatives. Mrs. Warren is reticent, then suddenly she drops the barriers of gentility, and defends her way of life as a brothel keeper. As Shaw notes in his stage directions, she has 'an overwhelming inspiration of true conviction and scorn in her' and Vivie's 'replies . . . now begin to ring rather woodenly and even priggishly against the new tone of her mother' (CP 75).

In this exchange Vivie learns that Mrs. Warren went into prostitution as a trade which offered more security and better conditions than others which were open to her as an uneducated working-class girl. Shaw is able to make his point strongly that there is something wrong with a society that rewards prostitution better than so-called honest work, but one wonders whether he makes prostitution sound too attractive in his anxiety to condemn those who operated a system that forced girls into jobs such as the whitelead factory where Mrs. Warren's sister worked 'twelve hours a day for nine shillings a week until she died of lead poisoning' (CP 75). He says little about the disadvantages of a career in prostitution. Nothing is mentioned of disease or the brutality of the pimps who are invariably connected with the business. The nearest Shaw comes to outright criticism of the job is in a speech by Mrs. Warren towards the end of the act:

> Everybody dislikes having to work and make money; but they have to do it all the same. I'm sure Ive often pitied a poor girl, tired out and in low spirits, having to try to please some man that she doesnt care two straws for—some half-drunken fool that thinks he's making himself agreeable when he's teasing and worrying and disgusting a woman so that hardly any money could pay her for

putting up with it. But she has to bear with disagreeables and take the rough with the smooth, just like a nurse in a hospital or anyone else. It's not work that any woman would do for pleasure, goodness knows; though to hear the pious people talk you would suppose it was a bed of roses.   CP 76

Shaw only tells part of the truth here, since his purpose is not to write a wholly realistic play. The equation of the work of a prostitute with that of 'a nurse in a hospital' reinforces the fact that Shaw's chief aim in *Mrs. Warren's Profession* is to cause his mainly middle-class audience to reconsider all their accepted ideas about the employment of women, who were generally exploited at the time.

Act Two ends with Vivie having gained a new respect for her mother because of the honesty with which her case has been presented, but it is important to note that she believes the events described by Mrs. Warren to be over and done with.

However, in the following scenes Vivie learns that her mother still continues to manage a chain of continental brothels, with Sir George Crofts as her chief shareholder. Crofts tells her this when she refuses his offer of marriage and she is deflated when she learns that her Cambridge education was paid for with money from the business. She is forced to admit 'You might go on to point out that I myself never asked where the money I spent came from. I believe I am just as bad as you' (Act Three CP 83).

Crofts is galled by Vivie's attitude of horror at his revelations and in a fit of pique tells Vivie and Frank of their relationship as half-brother and sister. Act Three ends with Vivie going off to the City to work for herself in order to gain independence from her mother and her tainted source of income.

The mood of the final act is muted. We discover Vivie, two days after the events of Act Three, in her City office happily working for her living. In the course of the act she receives visits from Frank, Praed and her mother. Frank tries to persuade Vivie that nothing has altered and he tells her that his father denies Crofts' allegation. When Praed comes in it becomes clear that neither he nor Frank realises the source of Mrs. Warren's income, and in a melodramatic but effective way, Vivie informs the two men by passing a note to them disclosing what she cannot bring herself to speak. Frank, ever practical, realises that he cannot now accept an allowance from Mrs. Warren and leaves Vivie a note 'withdrawing gracefully and leaving the field to the gilded youth of England' (Act Four CP 88).

The stage is set for the final confrontation between Mrs. Warren and Vivie. Mrs. Warren first tries to tempt Vivie with the idea of the power that money can bring and then tells her that if she had realised that Vivie would grow up independent she would have placed her as a prostitute in one of her own brothels. The scene is riveting and one can feel sympathy for both women, particularly for Mrs. Warren who is harshly made to realise that she has no rights as a mother over Vivie. The play ends with Vivie settling down in independence to work, but we are left with Mrs. Warren's words ringing in our ears: 'Oh, the injustice of it! the injustice! the injustice! I always wanted to be a good woman. I tried honest work; and I was slave-driven until I cursed the day I ever heard of honest work' (Act Four CP 92). Shaw insists that we remember that all Mrs. Warren's transgressions stem from social conditions.

Certain incidents and attitudes expressed in *Mrs. Warren's Profession* echo those found in *Widowers' Houses*. In the big scene in which Mrs. Warren explains to her daughter, Vivie, why she went into prostitution Shaw brilliantly brings out the wretchedness of the prospects for any girl of the working class at the time he was writing about, and he does so in a way that makes us think twice about condemning Sartorius in *Widowers' Houses*. Trench in the one play and Vivie in the other become *our* representatives in the arguments. At first, like us, they are revolted at the knowledge of how their elders make their money. Vivie is supercilious, saying, 'People are always blaming their circumstances for what they are. I dont believe in circumstances. The people who get on in this world are the people who get up and look for the circumstances they want, and, if they cant find them, make them' (Act Two CP 75). When Vivie tells Crofts that she is as bad as he is we are immediately reminded of Trench's comment when he learns from Sartorius that his income is derived from a mortgage on the latter's property—'Do you mean to say that I am just as bad as you are?' (Act Two CP 18).

There are other echoes and parallels in the two plays, among the most striking of which is the fact that in the end Trench and Vivie are much harder in attitude than Sartorius and Mrs. Warren, although it could be argued that Vivie is unbending from the beginning. *Widowers' Houses* ends on an extremely depressing note with Trench cynically ready to look on the repair of slum property 'as simply a question of so much money' when earlier he had been so shocked by the revelation of the source of his income.

Even though I have drawn attention to some of the reasons why these plays deserve a higher reputation than they have had during the past seventy years, we cannot overlook the fact that they contain flaws which mark them as the work of a dramatist learning his trade. We note for instance a clumsiness in the contrivance of exits and entrances, and occasionally the plot is helped on by the long arm of coincidence. For example, the Reverend Samuel Gardner is brought up against a reminder of his unrespectable past in the shape of Mrs. Warren at the end of the first act of *Mrs. Warren's Profession*, and in *Widowers' Houses* and *The Philanderer* vital information can only be conveyed by the delivery of a bluebook and the *British Medical Journal*. We might also cavil at the transformation of Lickcheese from a down-trodden rent collector into a man of property at the end of *Widowers' Houses*. It is an effective theatrical trick (one that Shaw was to use again in *Pygmalion* with the transformation of Doolittle, the dustman) but judged from the point of view of likelihood it is difficult to accept.

'PLAYS PLEASANT'

In the Preface to *Plays Unpleasant* Shaw writes:

> Finally, a word as to why I have labelled the three plays in this first volume Unpleasant. The reason is pretty obvious: their dramatic power is used to force the spectator to face unpleasant facts. No doubt all plays which deal sincerely with humanity must wound the monstrous conceit which it is the business of romance to flatter.
>
> CPBS 726

This last sentence is the key to the way in which we should read those plays which appear in the companion volume to *Plays Unpleasant—Plays Pleasant*, which appeared in 1898. Just as Shaw had seen the necessity of examining the sources of middle-class wealth in *Widowers' Houses* and *Mrs. Warren's Profession*, so he decided that subjects usually treated in an unrealistic, romantic way in the theatre should be looked at clear-sightedly in *Plays Pleasant*. In the Preface he tells us that 'idealism, which is only a flattering name for romance in politics and morals, is as obnoxious to me as romance in ethics or religion' (CPBS 734). In *Plays Pleasant* romance is not victorious. We are shown a cowardly soldier in *Arms and the Man*; *Candida* concerns a wife who prefers to remain with her somewhat dull husband rather than evade her responsibilities by going off with a young poet; while *You Never Can Tell* shows Shaw's Life Force in action when Gloria Clandon forces the reluctant Valentine to marry her.

A later chapter is concerned with recurrent comic techniques used by Shaw in his plays. In the discussions which follow of *Arms and the Man* and *Candida* some points will be mentioned that are to be developed more fully later. Here I am concerned mainly with stressing the anti-romantic qualities common to *Plays Unpleasant* and *Plays Pleasant*.

'*Arms and the Man*'

Arms and the Man was produced in 1894, and was Shaw's first success in the theatre. It was staged earlier than Shaw intended, owing to the unexpected failure of a double-bill produced at the Avenue Theatre by the actress Florence Farr. Shaw put the finishing touches to his own play, and set about finding suitable actors for the parts. Writing to one actress whom he hoped to persuade to undertake the part of Raina, he refers to the part of Blanche, in *Widowers' Houses*:

> The lady does not swear, nor does she throttle the servant like the heroine in my other play. She has to make herself a little ridiculous (unconsciously) once or twice; but for the most part she has to be romantically beautiful or else amusing in a bearably dignified way. She is a Bulgarian, and can, I suppose, wear extraordinary things if she wishes.　　　　　　　　　Letter to Alma Murray, 30 March 1894

However, just as Blanche's attack on her servant-girl had upset many readers, as well as members of the audiences who attended the first private performances of *Widowers' Houses*, so *Arms and the Man* also caused offence in some quarters, although we today would consider the criticism of warfare that the play contains to be understated, if anything.

Shaw wrote in a letter to William Archer on 23 April 1894:

> I do not accept the conventional ideals. To them I oppose in the play the practical life & morals of the efficient, realistic man, unaffectedly ready to face what risks must be faced, considerate but not chivalrous, patient and practical.

It is with 'the practical life and morals of the efficient, realistic man' that the play is chiefly concerned, and it achieves its effects because of the seriousness of some of Shaw's comments set against its 'comic-opera' background. (Incidentally, *Arms and the Man* was used as the basis of the operetta, *The Chocolate Soldier*, by Oscar Strauss.)

The play opens in the bedroom of Raina, the daughter of Major Petkoff of the Bulgarian army. In the first speeches we are told (along with Raina) that the Bulgarians have beaten the Serbs at the Battle of Slivnitza. It appears that the victory has been achieved as a result of a cavalry charge led by Raina's fiancé, Sergius Saranoff. In view of what is to happen later it is interesting to note that even so early in the play Shaw shows us that Raina has not always been a wholly committed romantic idealist:

RAINA: I am so happy! so proud! (*She rises and walks about excitedly*). It proves that all our ideas were real after all.

CATHERINE (*indignantly*): Our ideas real! What do you mean?

RAINA: Our ideas of what Sergius would do. Our patriotism. Our heroic ideals. I sometimes used to doubt whether they were anything but dreams. Oh, what faithless little creatures girls are! When I buckled on Sergius's sword he looked so noble: it was treason to think of disillusion or humiliation or failure. And yet—and yet— (*She sits down again suddenly*) Promise me youll never tell him.

CATHERINE: Dont ask me for promises until I know what I'm promising.

RAINA: Well, it came into my head just as he was holding me in his arms and looking into my eyes that perhaps we only had our heroic ideas because we are so fond of reading Byron and Pushkin, and because we were so delighted with the opera that season at Bucharest. ACT ONE CP 93

In *Arms and the Man* Shaw is going to show us the futility of heroic ideas, and we shall be reminded in the last act of Raina's 'Oh, what faithless little creatures girls are!'

When her mother and Louka, the maid, leave the room, Raina goes to bed, having first elevated the portrait of Sergius 'like a priestess'. Her words, 'My hero! my hero!' (Act One CP 94) show that she is once more back in the world of heroism derived from the opera and romantic poetry. At this point in the play, however, realism enters in the shape of a fleeing Serb officer, Captain Bluntschli, who climbs into Raina's bedroom to escape from the pursuing Bulgarian soldiers.

Bluntschli, who is not at this point named, represents the anti-romantic view of war, in fact the anti-romantic view of everything. He holds Raina at pistol point, and tells her that he does not intend to get killed if he can help it. She reverts to her second-hand ideas of the glory of war:

RAINA: *Some* soldiers, I know, are *afraid* to die. ACT ONE CP 95

Bluntschli's reply is blunt, as his name would suggest:

All of them, dear lady, all of them, believe me. It is our duty to live as long as we can. ACT ONE CP 95

This answer, perfectly acceptable to people today, who know of the horrors of two World Wars, was revolutionary at the time the play was written. It sets the mood for further anti-romantic revelations from the intruder. Bluntschli tells Raina that he fights for a living, not because of patriotic motives:

Dont hate me, dear young lady. I am a Swiss, fighting merely as a professional soldier. I joined the Serbs because they came first on the road from Switzerland. ACT ONE CP 96

The down-to-earth note that is struck here is echoed in Bluntschli's statement that he carries chocolate instead of

36

cartridges when he goes into battle. Raina scornfully gives him the remainder of a box of chocolate creams which he devours ravenously, saying:

> Bless you, dear lady! You can always tell an old soldier by the inside of his holsters and cartridge boxes. The young ones carry pistols and cartridges: the old ones, grub.   ACT ONE CP 97

This first act is seen therefore as a contrast between realism and idealism. Raina romantically conceals Bluntschli behind the curtains, even though he is an enemy, and she tells him that he would have been safe if, instead of threatening her with a pistol, he had simply thrown himself as a fugitive on the Petkoffs' sense of hospitality. It is an idea that she has gained from the opera of *Ernani*. To contrast with Raina's girlish notions of how nations make war, however, Shaw insists on Bluntschli's exhaustion, as he has not closed his eyes for forty-eight hours, and the first act ends with his falling asleep on Raina's bed.

The remaining two acts of the play take place four months later. In Act Two we are introduced to Raina's father, Major Petkoff, and her fiancé, Sergius. Sergius and Petkoff describe to Raina and her mother the conduct of a Swiss officer they met at an exchange of prisoners. Petkoff asks Sergius to tell the ladies the story of the Swiss soldier's escape after Slivnitza. The tale is highly embarrassing to Raina and her mother:

SERGIUS: To escape their sabres he climbed a waterpipe and made his way into the bedroom of a young Bulgarian lady. The young lady was enchanted by his persuasive commercial traveller's manners. She very modestly entertained him for an hour or so, and then called in her mother lest her conduct should appear unmaidenly. The old lady was equally fascinated; and the fugitive was sent on his way in the morning, disguised in an old coat belonging to the master of the house, who was away at the war.   ACT TWO CP 105

Raina and Catherine pretend to be shocked by the coarseness of the story.

Obviously the old coat referred to in Sergius's speech quoted above is going to play an important part in the plot. Towards the end of Act Two Captain Bluntschli arrives to return it, and Raina and her mother are forced into subterfuge to keep their secret from Major Petkoff. He, however, is glad to see Bluntschli, who can help him in practical matters about arranging for three cavalry regiments to be sent to Philippopolis.

The final act of the play sees Raina and Sergius switch their affections away from one another. Sergius has already in Act Two flirted with Louka, Raina's servant, as he finds Raina's notions of the higher love 'very fatiguing . . . to keep up for any length of time' (CP 106). The secret of Act One is revealed to Major Petkoff and Sergius, and the latter challenges Bluntschli to a duel. Once more the anti-romantic streak in Bluntschli is shown by the way in which he reacts:

BLUNTSCHLI (*staring, but sitting quite at his ease*): Oh, thank you: thats a
    cavalry man's proposal. I'm in the artillery; and I have the choice
    of weapons. If I go, I shall take a machine gun. And there shall
    be no mistake about the cartridges this time.   ACT THREE CP 117

There are several clearly-marked points in Act Three to prepare us for Raina's acceptance of Bluntschli as a husband. When he tells her that he will not hurt Sergius in the duel, he concludes, 'It will save explanations. In the morning I shall be off home; and youll never see me or hear of me again. You and he will then make it up and live happily ever after' (CP 117). Raina's reaction to this speech is significant:

RAINA (*turning away deeply hurt, almost with a sob in her voice*): I never said
    I wanted to see you again.   ACT THREE CP 117

She also reacts favourably when Bluntschli reveals that he has what he terms 'an incurably romantic disposition' (CP 121), and he then makes a proposal for her hand in marriage, Sergius having renounced Raina to become engaged to Louka.

The play ends on a note of inspired foolery. The Petkoffs are not keen on their daughter marrying, as they think, beneath her. Bluntschli is forced to parade the wealth he has inherited from his father, a Swiss hotel-keeper. His exchange with Sergius is always supremely effective in the theatre:

38

BLUNTSCHLI: Oh well, if it comes to a question of an establishment, here goes! (*He darts impetuously to the table; seizes the papers in the blue envelope; and turns to Sergius.*)

How many horses did you say?

SERGIUS: Twenty, noble Switzer.

BLUNTSCHLI: I have two hundred horses. (*They are amazed.*) How many carriages?

SERGIUS: Three.

BLUNTSCHLI: I have seventy. Twenty-four of them will hold twelve inside, besides two on the box, without counting the driver and conductor. How many tablecloths have you?

SERGIUS: How the deuce do I know?

BLUNTSCHLI: Have you four thousand?

SERGIUS: No.

BLUNTSCHLI: I have. I have nine thousand six hundred pairs of sheets and blankets, with two thousand four hundred eider-down quilts. I have ten thousand knives and forks, and the same quantity of dessert spoons. I have three hundred servants. I have six palatial establishments, besides two livery stables, a tea gardens, and a private house. I have four medals for distinguished services; I have the rank of an officer and the standing of a gentleman; and I have three native languages. Shew me any man in Bulgaria that can offer as much! ACT THREE CP 122

The hammer-blow reiteration of 'I have' reduces the others on stage to awe-struck reverence, and the audience to helpless laughter in a good production.

Arms and the Man is basically a light-hearted play, but what we retain after reading or seeing it is not only a pleasurable feeling from having experienced a witty piece of writing. At every point possible Shaw pricks the bubble of false romanticism. He shows us that Raina's ideas of the battlefield are inaccurate by letting Bluntschli tell her of the realities. He shows that Sergius needs to make love to the maid, as he finds the higher love too fatiguing. To reinforce further the idea of romantic attitudes about love being deluded, he shows Major Petkoff's servant, Nicola, ready to give up his fiancée, Louka, for profit:

NICOLA: Ive often thought that if Raina were out of the way, and you just a little less of a fool and Sergius just a little more of one,

39

> you might come to be one of my grandest customers, instead of
> only being my wife and costing me money.
>
> LOUKA: I believe you would rather be my servant than my husband.
> You would make more out of me. ACT THREE CP 115

The play concentrates on attitudes that were not popular in the Victorian theatre, although few modern readers would be shocked by it. Nevertheless, it is worth noting that Shaw's friend, William Archer, wrote of *Arms and the Man*:

> Mr. Shaw is by nature and habit one of those philosophers who concentrate their attention upon the seamy side of the human mind. . . . He not only dwells on the seamy side to the exclusion of all else, but he makes his characters turn their moral garments inside out and go about with the linings displayed, flaunting the seams and raw edges and stiffenings and paddings. *The World* 25 April 1894

It is hard to agree with this assessment, but Archer hints here in an interesting way at a technique which Shaw was to use through-out his career. By 'turn their moral garments inside out' he appears to be referring to the way in which the characters behave in unexpected ways. This use of paradox in Shaw is examined at greater length in Chapter Five.

'Candida'

Candida was the next of the *Plays Pleasant* to be written. It was completed in December 1894 and yet did not achieve its first public performances in England until 1904. Since that time it has been one of the most frequently revived of Shaw's plays, largely because it has all the commercial qualities that Shaw himself ascribes to it in a letter, written on 22 February 1895, to the actor, Richard Mansfield, who was considering producing the play in America:

> Now let me ask you whether you can play a boy of eighteen—a strange creature—a poet—a bundle of nerves—a genius—and a rattling good part. The actor-managers here can't get down to the age. The play, which is called *Candida*, is the most fascinating work in the world—my latest—in three acts, one cheap scene, and with six characters. The woman's part divides the interest and the necessary genius with the poet's.

The play is chiefly of interest to us today because of the presentation of the poet Eugene Marchbanks, and Candida's reactions to him. Candida is the thirtythree-year-old wife of the Reverend James Morell, and Marchbanks is one of Morell's discoveries—'He found him sleeping on the Embankment last June' (Act One CP 130). Thus, from the beginning, the 'romantic' qualities of Marchbanks are stressed.

The poet tells Morell that he has fallen in love with his wife, and, towards the end of Act Two, Candida informs her husband that Marchbanks needs her love:

CANDIDA: I mean, will he forgive me for not teaching him myself? For abandoning him to the bad women for the sake of my goodness, of my purity, as you call it? Ah, James, how little you understand me, to talk of your confidence in my goodness and purity! I would give them both to poor Eugene as willingly as I would give my shawl to a beggar dying of cold, if there were nothing else to restrain me.   ACT TWO CP 141

All seems set for Candida to leave her husband for Marchbanks, but, forced to choose between them, she gives herself 'to the weaker of the two' (Act Three CP 151), who is, paradoxically, her husband. Marchbanks is shown to have matured almost instantaneously in the last moments of the play when, as Candida says, 'he has learnt to live without happiness' (Act Three CP 152).

Just as Shaw defeated the expectations of his audience in *Mrs. Warren's Profession* and *Arms and the Man*, giving them instead of the golden-hearted prostitute and the dashing warrior of the popular stage, the business woman and the chocolate cream soldier, so in *Candida* he reverses the expected ending to the play. In the 'romantic' theatre Candida and Eugene would have gone away together, but Candida herself realises the impossibility of this happening:

CANDIDA: Will you, for my sake, make a little poem out of the two sentences I am going to say to you? And will you promise to repeat it to yourself whenever you think of me?
MARCHBANKS (*without moving*): Say the sentences.
CANDIDA: When I am thirty, she will be forty-five. When I am sixty, she will be seventy-five.   ACT THREE CP 152

At other points in the play the audience is led to expect this rejection. Marchbanks is unable to see the necessity for mundane work in this life. In Act Two he lets forth 'a heart-breaking wail' when Candida mentions that her 'own particular pet scrubbing brush has been used for blackleading' (CP 138–9). Candida realises that he has been upset by the linking of the scrubbing brush and herself, and asks him if he would like to present her with a new one 'with an ivory back inlaid with mother-of-pearl' (CP 139). His answer, and Morell's comment upon it, force the audience to reject Marchbanks and what he stands for:

MARCHBANKS (*softly and musically, but sadly and longingly*): No, not a scrubbing brush, but a boat: a tiny shallop to sail away in, far from the world, where the marble floors are washed by the rain and dried by the sun; where the south wind dusts the beautiful green and purple carpets. Or a chariot! to carry us up into the sky, where the lamps are stars, and dont need to be filled with paraffin oil every day.

MORELL (*harshly*): And where there is nothing to do but to be idle, selfish, and useless. ACT TWO CP 139

A few lines earlier, Shaw has caused a laugh at Marchbanks's expense by allowing Candida's father, the down-to-earth Mr. Burgess, to misinterpret his cry of 'Only horror! horror! horror!' (CP 139) at the thought of Candida scrubbing floors. Burgess automatically assumes that Marchbanks's horrors are caused by drinking, and urges him to leave it off gradually. One is forced to the conclusion that Shaw was unable to resist poking fun at one who represented the point of view of 'Art for Art's sake'. Yet there remains the letter to Richard Mansfield, quoted above; does he mean it when he calls Marchbanks a genius, or is he merely trying to attract a first-class actor to play in *Candida*?

In *Plays Unpleasant* and *Plays Pleasant* Shaw lays the foundations for his writing for the theatre. The chief characteristic of these early plays is his delight in reversal of the normally expected. This technique of the use of paradox is something to which I shall return in Chapter Five.

3

Shaw and Evolution

In the previous chapter we observed how Shaw saw the theatre as a means of improving social conditions, and how in plays such as *Mrs. Warren's Profession* he examined specific social problems of the late 19th century. As a result of these plays injustices were brought before a wider audience than would otherwise have been perturbed by them, as dramatic representation has long been recognised as capable of bringing problems to life in a more vivid way than any other yet discovered.

Shaw was not content, however, merely to present problems which could be solved by reforms in social justice. He saw that Man himself must wish to change for the better before life could begin to be enjoyable for the vast majority of mankind. Having read widely in the writings of 19th-century biologists and philosophers, Shaw came to the conclusion that the purpose behind Nature could be called Creative Evolution. Briefly, according to Shaw, the aim of Creative Evolution is that Nature (using her highest work so far—Man) is striving for self-awareness and self-knowledge. When this is attained, if it ever can be, Man will be able to live happily without strife or vice, and Nature's purpose will be on the way to being fulfilled. Complete fulfilment will be attained when humanity shall have passed away, leaving behind only pure thought—which is the essence of Nature.

At least three of Shaw's plays (if we count *Back to Methuselah* as one play) are primarily concerned with exploration of the subject of Creative Evolution, while several other plays contain incidental references to it. It would be a mistake to think that *Man and Superman*, *Back to Methuselah* and *The Simpleton of the*

Unexpected Isles deal exclusively with the doctrine of Creative Evolution, but it is on this aspect of the plays that we shall concentrate in this chapter.

Man and Superman is a play on the Don Juan theme, written by Shaw at the suggestion of his friend, A. B. Walkley (the dramatic critic). We gather from the Preface, which takes the form of an open letter to Walkley, that, characteristically, Shaw is going to treat the Don Juan theme paradoxically. Instead of showing us a Don Juan who pursues women, he is going to use the play to illustrate his ideas of Creative Evolution. His Don Juan is to be ensnared by a woman against his conscious will, showing that woman is the prime mover in Nature's purpose: she needs man in order to help her breed and so she will use all her wiles to trap him. It is in the working out of this plot that the comedy of *Man and Superman* lies, but it would be a mistake to see the play merely as an amusing trifle.

Shaw has taken all the ingredients of the Don Juan legend, as used by Mozart in his opera *Don Giovanni*, and re-ordered them to write a four-act play which is very seldom performed in full, owing to its length. He has brought the story up to date, making Don Juan into John Tanner, a member of the English middle class. In the course of the play he gives us many parallels with the Don Juan story but we are always conscious of the new, entirely Shavian twist of having Don Juan pursued by the Doña Ana figure, Ann Whitefield.

Unfortunately, owing to the fact that Act Three, containing what is commonly known as the 'Don Juan in Hell' scene, is almost always omitted in performance, the play loses its philosophical core in the theatre. Shaw must take some of the blame for this himself, since, in his Preface, he writes of 'thrusting into my perfectly modern three-act play a totally extraneous act in which my hero, enchanted by the air of the Sierra, has a dream in which his Mozartian ancestor appears and philosophizes at great length in a Shavio-Socratic dialogue with the lady, the statue, and the devil' (CPBS 154). As we shall see when we consider the play, the Hell scene is by no means 'extraneous'. To remove it does not exactly make nonsense of the rest of the play, but it certainly diminishes it in stature. However, until English theatregoers are prepared to spend as long sitting at a play as music lovers will spend at a performance of a Wagner opera most people will only know the full *Man and Superman* in book form.

The first act of *Man and Superman* is among the most perfect things Shaw ever wrote. It is high comedy of an order only to be found equalled by *The Importance of Being Earnest* among plays written in the last hundred years, and yet it also contains ideas. In fact it can be said that the comedy of the first act exists largely because of the ideas, although Shaw does not ignore other methods of making his play work theatrically.

We are introduced immediately to two of the most important characters, Roebuck Ramsden, an elderly business man, and Octavius Robinson, a young man in mourning clothes. At once Shaw makes it evident by the tone these two adopt in talking of their grief over the death of the late Mr. Whitefield, that we are not to take his death too seriously. We learn that the dead man has left two daughters (only one of whom we see in the play), and that Octavius Robinson and his sister Violet are his adopted children. It soon becomes apparent that Octavius, who is a young man of poetic temperament, is in love with Ann Whitefield and hopes to marry her, although the very impractical cast of mind that Shaw gives to Octavius warns the reader almost from the outset that this will not happen. Roebuck Ramsden believes that he is to be made trustee and guardian of Ann and her sister Rhoda, and lets Octavius know that under these circumstances he will not allow Octavius's friend, John Tanner, the author of an anarchistic pamphlet, to come into contact with the two young women. The irony of this is that Ramsden has himself been something of a revolutionary thinker in his day and still considers himself to have advanced opinions. At this point we are told that Tanner has just arrived at Ramsden's house in company with Ann, her mother and Violet Robinson.

The entry of Tanner causes the play to burst into life. In a state of panic he waves a copy of Mr. Whitefield's will under Ramsden's nose and to our amusement we learn that he has been appointed, with Ramsden, joint guardian of Ann; they are equally horrified at being thus linked together. In the following speeches we see that Tanner has a much more realistic idea of Ann than Octavius has, and, although we have already been told that he is afraid of Ann, Shaw points the way to what is to be the outcome when he makes Tanner say 'I might as well be her husband' (Act One CP 336).

The dialogue from this point onwards is scintillating. Shaw makes Tanner the spokesman for many of his own provocative ideas and the speeches he gives to him are brilliantly built up, almost in the form of operatic arias. It is as though Tanner can be triggered off into an exciting flow of ideas on almost any subject, but chiefly he is ready to speak of the position of the artist in society and the function of woman in the world. When Tanner and Octavius are left alone for a while Shaw brings to the fore, for the first time in the play, the Evolution theme. Tanner tells Octavius that '[woman's] purpose is neither her happiness nor yours, but Nature's. Vitality in a woman is a blind fury of creation' (Act One CP 340). He goes on to say that man is only useful to woman as a breeder and protector for the young. This is something to which Shaw will return in the Hell scene.

Now Shaw introduces the second strand to his plot with the story of Octavius's sister, Violet. By an amusing series of misunderstandings Ann, Ramsden, Tanner and the others are led to believe that Violet has become pregnant while still unmarried. The general reaction is one of shocked despair, but Tanner, ever ready to defend his own advanced views, is delighted by the fact that (as he thinks) Nature is directing operations:

'Good Heavens, man, what are you crying for? Here is a woman whom we all supposed to be making bad water color sketches, practising Grieg and Brahms, gadding about to concerts and parties, wasting her life and her money. We suddenly learn that she had turned from these sillinesses to the fulfilment of her highest purpose and greatest function—to increase, multiply, and replenish the earth.' ACT ONE CP 342

He is scathing towards those who are ready to despise Violet and offers to help her financially. After an amusing quarrel sequence between Tanner and Ramsden the latter goes up to the drawing room to explain what is to be done to help Violet in her supposed distress. Ann and Tanner are left alone.

Earlier in the act Ann has called Tanner 'Don Juan', and we now see more clearly the relationships of the characters with those of the old legend. The positions of Ann, Tanner and Octavius are quite clear and it would appear that Ramsden, Ann's guardian, acting as the father substitute figure, is to play the part of the father of Doña Ana. Certainly his opposition to Tanner could not be more strongly emphasised, so we are prepared for the parts to be taken by Ann, Tanner and Ramsden in the Hell scene.

In the duologue between Ann and Tanner in the second half of Act One, we see that she is out to fascinate him and it becomes clear that this Don Juan is a marked victim, although he does not realise it himself. Ann, the representative of woman ready to fulfil Nature's purpose, sees in him her prospective mate, and is quite ready to ignore Tanner's opinions so long as she is able to capture him. She tells him that she is too feminine to see any sense in destruction, and it is obvious to us that Tanner is right when he says, 'Thats because you confuse construction and destruction with creation and murder' (Act One CP 346). Ann is definitely the instrument of Nature's creative purpose.

As the scene proceeds Jack feels Ann's fascination, but thinks mistakenly that she is merely playing with him, and that her real designs are upon Octavius. He is unable to see what Ann means when she says 'I wonder are you really a clever man!' but the audience can see what is going to happen.

After this interlude the play once again returns to the other action of the plot, that concerning Violet Robinson, whom we have not yet seen. Act One ends on a rising note with everyone including Tanner put down by Violet. It appears that she is not in need of help or pity; in fact, she indignantly rejects them, as she is a married woman. Her horror at being approved of by Tanner, whose opinions she abhors, causes her to reveal her clandestine marriage and he is very deflated. Shaw saves his master stroke

47

until almost the end of the scene when it is revealed that Ann knew about Violet's marriage from the beginning. We are bound to echo Tanner's cry, 'Oh!!! Unfathomable deceit! Double crossed!' (CP 350).

The act ends with a crestfallen group 'cowering before the wedding ring' (CP 351), but we still do not know who is Violet's husband. That will be revealed in Act Two.

The second act is more relaxed in tone than the first, and serves as a kind of resting place between its excitements and the intellectually testing debates of Act Three. It is chiefly important for two things; it introduces us to Tanner's chauffeur, Enry Straker, and in it we learn that Violet is married to the young American, Hector Malone.

Straker is a representative of that stock figure of comedy, the knowing, managing servant who is able to score off his master. The line goes back through Molière to classical comedy. Shaw, however, makes use of Straker to express his views on education and progress in society. The public schools are derided when set against the board school 'where boys learn something' (CP 352), and the emphasis that Shaw placed on the utility of education can be seen from the following exchange between Tanner and his servant:

TANNER: You despise Oxford, Enry, dont you?
STRAKER: No, I dont. Very nice sort of place, Oxford, I should think, for people that like that sort of place. They teach you to be a gentleman there. In the Polytechnic they teach you to be an engineer or such like. See?
TANNER: Sarcasm, Tavy, sarcasm! Oh, if you could only see into Enry's soul, the depth of his contempt for a gentleman, the arrogance of his pride in being an engineer, would appal you. He positively likes the car to break down because it brings out my gentlemanly helplessness and his workmanlike skill and resource.

ACT TWO CP 352

Straker is a hardheaded Socialist who remains unimpressed when Octavius says 'I believe most intensely in the dignity of labor'. His reply is at once comic and true:

48

STRAKER: Thats because you never done any, Mr. Robinson. My business is to do away with labor. Youll get more out of me and a machine than you will out of twenty laborers, and not so much to drink either.   ACT TWO CP 352

Straker acts knowingly throughout the scene whenever Ann's name is mentioned. He realises long before Tanner does that she has marked him down for her mate. All of Tanner's remarks to Tavy in this scene comparing the behaviour of women to mating insects are comic to the audience because we realise, while he does not, that Ann is the pursuer and he is the pursued. However, Shaw means these reflections on the functions of the artist and of woman to be taken seriously. As he says, the business of the woman is to get married, while the artist has his art to satisfy him. Tanner puts it as follows:

> 'By Heaven, Tavy, if women could do without our work, and we ate their children's bread instead of making it, they would kill us as the spider kills her mate or as the bees kill the drone. And they would be right if we were good for nothing but love.'
>
> ACT TWO CP 354

Later in the act we see how Ann is scheming to capture Tanner. She uses excuses about his revolutionary views to prevent his being alone with her sister, and manages to evade the blame by laying the responsibility for the decision on her mother. This leads to an impassioned speech by Tanner in which Shaw allows himself to ride his hobbyhorse about the position of women in polite society. It leaves Ann unmoved as she considers he is merely speechmaking, but, to Tanner's horror, she takes him at his word when he tries to make her break the chains of respectability and flee with him across Africa. When the other characters enter she traps him by saying that he has offered to take her to Nice by motor car. He cannot, of course, openly deny this.

It is at this point that Shaw introduces Hector Malone. Malone suggests that the travelling party to Nice shall be extended and offers to take Violet. He is warned by Tanner and Octavius that Violet is already married and appears thunderstruck by the information. However, a little while later, we gather that

Ds   49

Hector is, in fact, Violet's husband, although the marriage must still be kept secret because of his father's attitude towards the English middle class.

Act Two ends on a note of great urgency when Straker lets Tanner know that Miss Whitefield is not interested in Octavius 'cause she's arter summun else'.

TANNER (*wildly appealing to the heavens*): Then I—I am the bee, the spider, the marked down victim, the destined prey.

STRAKER: I dunno about the bee and the spider. But the marked down victim, thats what you are and no mistake; and a jolly good job for you, too, I should say.   ACT TWO CP 360

A staccato exchange occurs between master and man as Tanner seeks to escape from his unwanted destiny. He commands Straker to drive him 'away like mad to Marseilles, Gibraltar, Genoa, any port from which we can sail to a Mahometan country where men are protected from women' (CP 361). Ann has been shown in this scene moving in for the kill, but Tanner is not going to succumb without a fight.

Bandits and the 'Don Juan in Hell' Scene

A common accusation levelled against Shaw by those who do not like his plays is that he did not write plays, but sermons and debates. They claim that there is no action in his writing and this is true of much of his later work, where the talk does sometimes seem to flow on interminably in a way that is not dramatic. These critics were first given ammunition by Shaw's third act in *Man and Superman*, but only a superficial reader will find it uninteresting.

Tanner, endeavouring to escape from Ann, is being driven across Spain by Straker when they are ambushed by a band of most unlikely brigands led by one Mendoza. The criminals remind us of the supporters of Captain Brassbound (in *Captain Brassbound's Conversion*) and afford Shaw ample opportunities for amusing (yet serious) commentary on the reasons that make men paupers or tramps. In his long stage direction at the beginning of Act Three, he defends those who will not put up with dull, ill-paid work offering no scope for the imagination, and suggests that by becoming paupers they are merely exploiting a society that exploits them in a more shameful fashion. He continues: 'We may therefore contemplate the tramps of the Sierra without prejudice, admitting cheerfully that our objects—briefly, to be gentlemen of fortune—are much the same as theirs, and the difference in our position and methods merely accidental' (Act Three CP 362).

Mendoza's brigands are an unlikely lot who exist in a fairy-tale-like atmosphere. Shaw asks us to accept that they carry on debates on philosophical and political questions in the intervals of holding up travellers across the Sierra, but this is done so that the transition to the dream sequence (the 'Don Juan in Hell' scene) shall not seem too abrupt when it comes. Before the dream sequence begins, Shaw gives us some amusing paradoxical dialogue between Mendoza and Tanner:

MENDOZA (*with dignity*): Allow me to introduce myself: Mendoza, President of the League of the Sierra! (*Posing loftily*) I am a brigand: I live by robbing the rich.

TANNER (*promptly*): I am a gentleman: I live by robbing the poor. Shake hands.   ACT THREE CP 364

The two men are instantly at home with one another and talk in friendly fashion. Tanner is quite ready to pay any ransom that Mendoza should require, and when Mendoza says, 'You are a remarkable man, sir. Our guests usually describe themselves as miserably poor', he replies:

'Pooh! Miserably poor people dont own motor cars.'
                                        ACT THREE CP 364–5

In order to suspend disbelief still further, so that we shall accept the dream sequence more readily, Shaw makes Mendoza reveal a startling coincidence when he tells the story of his life to Tanner and Straker: it appears that he has taken to banditry as the result of being in love with Straker's sister, Louisa, a domestic servant, a fact which Enry takes rather badly. In this atmosphere we are prepared for anything to happen, particularly in view of the following lines just before Tanner and Straker fall asleep:

MENDOZA (*shaking his head*): The Sierra is no better than Bloomsbury
  when once the novelty has worn off. Besides, these mountains
  make you dream of women—of women with magnificent hair.
TANNER: Of Louisa, in short. They will not make me dream of women,
  my friend: I am heartwhole.
MENDOZA: Do not boast until morning, sir. This is a strange country for
  dreams.   ACT THREE CP 367

There follows the so-called extraneous section of the play in
which Shaw develops his ideas on Creative Evolution and a host
of other topics. Don Juan, Doña Ana, the Devil and the Statue
(who bear striking resemblances to Tanner, Ann, Mendoza and
Ramsden) are the participants in a long debate drama which
contains almost no physical action. However, it is always theatrical and never boring. In the Hell scene Shaw's rhetoric is at its
best, particularly in the speeches of Don Juan and the Devil, and
he shows the instinct of the true dramatist in never allowing his
audience to become bogged down in the argument. Often in the
course of the scene the statue of Doña Ana's father either refers
to the length of the speeches, or approves of the ideas expressed
or the way in which they are expressed, thus giving a sense of
movement to what is in fact very static drama from the physical
point of view, although the clash of ideas is extremely active.

The play within a play, as it has come to be regarded, begins in
typical Shavian fashion. Don Juan reveals to an old woman, who,
it later appears, is Doña Ana, that she is in Hell, a fact that
astounds and angers her. He tells her that Hell contains many
good people and that it is not the place she was led to believe it
would be. Shaw makes Don Juan state, in paradoxical fashion:

'You will be welcome in hell, Señora. Hell is the home of honor,
duty, justice, and the rest of the seven deadly virtues. All the
wickedness on earth is done in their name: where else but in hell
should they have their reward?'   ACT THREE CP 369

Shortly afterwards Shaw introduces his first hint of the
Evolution theme that is to take such a central position in this
scene. He looks forward to the argument he is to use later in
Back to Methuselah where he suggests that statesmen only attain

sufficient wisdom and experience to fit them for their task when they begin to decline physically because of old age:

DON JUAN: You forget that you have left your age behind you in the realm of time. You are no more 77 than you are 7 or 17 or 27.

THE OLD WOMAN: Nonsense!

DON JUAN: Consider, Señora: was not this true even when you lived on earth? When you were 70, were you really older underneath your wrinkles and your grey hairs than when you were 30?

THE OLD WOMAN: No, younger: at 30 I was a fool. But of what use is it to feel younger and look older?   ACT THREE CP 369–70

For the duration of the Hell scene the Old Woman chooses to appear as she was at twenty-seven, and is transformed into the figure of the young Doña Ana, who is the representation of Ann Whitefield in Tanner's dream. Immediately she and Don Juan recognise one another and the male-female love-hate relationship, that we have witnessed in earlier scenes between Tanner and Ann, once more gets under way.

In flippant style, Shaw prepares us for the entrance of the Statue of Doña Ana's father who, Don Juan informs her, 'condescends to look in upon us here from time to time. Heaven bores him' (CP 370).

We soon learn that the Statue envies Don Juan his freedom from hope in Hell and tells him that he has come to a momentous decision about which he must consult the Devil. Whereupon the Devil enters, looking 'not at all unlike Mendoza' (CP 372).

After his preliminary greetings to the company we learn that there exists extreme antipathy between the Devil and Don Juan. When the Statue informs the Devil of the momentous decision he referred to earlier, which is to leave Heaven and take up residence in Hell, the Devil wonders if the Statue cannot persuade Don Juan to take the place left vacant in Heaven. The Statue feels that he would find it too dull and uncomfortable. A little later the Statue, in a speech reminiscent of one by the English Soldier in the Epilogue to *Saint Joan*, tells his daughter that all the best people are in Hell, 'princes of the church and all. So few go to Heaven, and so many come here, that the blest, once called a heavenly host, are a continually dwindling minority' (CP 374).

However, the scene is chiefly famous for its qualities of rhetoric which are mainly demonstrated in a series of opposing speeches by the Devil and Don Juan. Briefly, it might be said that Don Juan is in favour of life, with all its attendant risks and discomforts, while the Devil is in favour of death. Shaw puts most of his evolutionary ideas into the speeches of Don Juan, but we must not imagine that the Devil's arguments are merely put up to be shot down by Don Juan. Some of the Devil's statements may be said to represent Shaw when he is being pessimistic about humanity, but the fact that Don Juan is so obviously the more admirable character shows that Shaw is basically optimistic in his point of view.

The debate between Don Juan and the Devil centres chiefly on the purpose behind nature. Don Juan sees Life as 'the force that ever strives to attain greater power of contemplating itself' and recognises that nature has endowed him with his brain in order that he shall not only be able to act, but know why he acts. Shaw makes Don Juan speak of the imperfections in Man's brains, but he goes on to contradict the Devil's assertion that 'One splendid body is worth the brains of a hundred dyspeptic, flatulent philosophers' (CP 375). The technique of the speech is very common in Shaw. He avoids monotony and accusations of lack of action by making his characters speak in statements, followed by a rhetorical question which in turn allows further statement:

DON JUAN: Things immeasurably greater than man in every respect but brain have existed and perished. The megatherium, the icthyosaurus have paced the earth with seven-league steps and hidden the day with cloud vast wings. Where are they now? Fossils in museums, and so few and imperfect at that, that a knuckle bone or a tooth of one of them is prized beyond the lives of a thousand soldiers. These things lived and wanted to live; but for lack of brains they did not know how to carry out their purpose, and so destroyed themselves. ACT THREE CP 375

The Devil, in equally magnificent prose, introduced by two rhetorical questions, argues that Man is not interested in life, but in death. He says that Man is supreme at inventing instruments of death and worships the force of death, which, he claims, touches the imagination. The speech in which the Devil expounds the attractiveness of Death for Man is Shaw at his best. It is built up with the care of a master craftsman and if we examine it we find that the rhythms of the writing depend on the use of the colon and the semi-colon and on the use of the rhetorical question:

THE DEVIL: This marvellous force of Life of which you boast is a force of Death: Man measures his strength by his destructiveness. What is his religion? An excuse for hating *me*. What is his law? An excuse for hanging *you*. What is his morality? Gentility! an excuse for consuming without producing. What is his art? An excuse for gloating over pictures of slaughter. What are his politics? Either the worship of a despot because a despot can kill, or parliamentary cock-fighting. . . . I saw a man die: he was a London bricklayer's laborer with seven children. He left seventeen pounds club money; and his wife spent it all on his funeral and went into the workhouse with the children next day. She would not have spent sevenpence on her children's schooling: the law had to force her to let them be taught gratuitously; but on death she spent all she had. Their imagination glows, their energies rise up at the idea of death, these people: they love it; and the more horrible it is the more they enjoy it.   ACT THREE CP 376

Don Juan refutes the Devil's picture of Man, saying that he will always fight for an idea. Once more when the debate appears to be going on without dramatic action Shaw gives the illusion of action by making an interruption by the Devil serve as a boost to get the talk going again:

THE DEVIL: Alas! Señor Commander, now that we have got on to the subject of Women, he will talk more than ever. However, I confess it is for me the one supremely interesting subject.

                                                              ACT THREE CP 378

Don Juan takes up the theme of Evolution once more, saying: 'Sexually, Woman is Nature's contrivance for perpetuating its highest achievement. Sexually, Man is Woman's contrivance for fulfilling Nature's behest in the most economical way' (CP 378). He sees Life as a force that is constantly making experiments to re-organise itself with the aim of 'driving at brains—at its darling object: an organ by which it can attain not only self-consciousness but self-understanding' (CP 379). Don Juan goes on to speak of his reason acting against his being trapped by 'the lady ... bent wholly on making sure of her prey' (CP 380). He says that he realised when he was on earth that Woman did not come up to the standards he had set for himself in his romantic illusions: '... my brain still said No on every issue. And whilst I was in the act of framing my excuse to the lady, Life seized me and threw me into her arms as a sailor throws a scrap of fish into the mouth of a seabird' (CP 381).

In a great display of aphorisms Don Juan goes on to talk of marriage as 'a mantrap' and 'the most licentious of human institutions', that being 'the secret of its popularity' (CP 382), and Shaw even allows the Statue to speak of the advantages of marriage and parenthood as a change from his usual references to the great length of Don Juan's speeches or the cleverness of the point in his arguments. Don Juan becomes even more brilliant in his rhetoric when he opposes Doña Ana's views on morality with his defence of the creative energy contained in the sex relation.

Shaw keeps his listeners amused in the midst of the rhetoric by exchanges such as that between the Statue and Don Juan when the former has already revealed that, in his younger days, he was a man for the ladies:

DON JUAN: And yet you, the hero of those scandalous adventures you have just been relating to us, *you* had the effrontery to pose as the avenger of outraged morality and condemn me to death! You would have slain me but for an accident.

THE STATUE: I was expected to, Juan. That is how things were arranged on earth. I was not a social reformer; and I always did what it was customary for a gentleman to do.   ACT THREE CP 385

This serves as a break before Shaw returns to the serious business of the scene. Don Juan tells the Devil 'that as long as I can conceive something better than myself I cannot be easy unless I am striving to bring it into existence or clearing the way for it' (CP 385). He speaks out against the lure of pleasures that the Devil offers, saying that the world must be improved even at the cost of personal discomfort. In a speech full of antitheses Don Juan insults those who follow the Devil, with the result that once more Shaw makes the Statue draw attention to his cleverness:

'Your flow of words is simply amazing, Juan.' ACT THREE CP 386

This is a trick he never forgot, as we can see when Amanda follows one of Magnus's great speeches in Act One of *The Apple Cart* with, 'You did speak that piece beautifully, sir' (CP 1026). It is always used as a cue for applause or approval.

The Devil tries to talk Don Juan out of his wish to depart for Heaven by telling him that there is no real progress behind Nature's apparent purpose, but Don Juan remains unconvinced. He feels that Man must 'be able to choose the line of greatest advantage instead of yielding in the direction of the least resistance' (CP 388). He reminds us of Captain Shotover in *Heartbreak House* when he says 'to be in hell is to drift: to be in heaven is to steer'.

We feel that perhaps Shaw is using the Devil as the mouthpiece for some of his own ideas in his long speech immediately prior to Don Juan's departure. In it the Devil speaks of the dangers of inoculation (one of Shaw's pet theories) and the corruption of politics, but he is only doing this to cast a golden glow on enjoyment as opposed to duty, and we know that Shaw's views are well represented by Don Juan, who looks on mindless pleasure with revulsion.

Don Juan goes and the Statue comments, 'Whew! How he does talk! Theyll never stand it in heaven' (CP 388).

The scene draws to a close amusingly with pantomime effects as the Statue and the Devil descend slowly into the bowels of Hell on a trapdoor, but even at this point Shaw does not entirely forsake his message. He makes the Devil speak of Nietzsche's idea of the Superman, who was to create his own morality and strike out in new directions rather than submit to the shackles of the morality of conventional civilisation based upon Christianity. Doña Ana reacts by asking where she can find the Superman. The Devil tells her that he has not yet been created and the Hell scene ends with Ana saying:

'Not yet created? Then my work is not yet done. (*Crossing herself devoutly*) I believe in the Life to Come. (*Crying to the universe*) A father! a father for the Superman!'

ACT THREE CP 389

In this scene Shaw is able to expand at length points at which he can only hint in the course of the modern comedy which surrounds it. As the scene takes the form of a dream we cannot ask for drama in the conventional sense of the word, but I hope enough has been said to convince the reader that Shaw never forgot his audience, even in this scene. Occasionally he can be silly, using cheap jokes and music hall effects, but despite this, we are treated to a display of wit, rhetoric and sheer information that can only set us thinking and admiring.

After the dream sequence the play takes up its interrupted course. Mendoza and his men are threatened with capture by Spanish soldiers, but Tanner saves them by saying that the brigands are his escort. Meanwhile another car arrives, bearing Ann Whitefield and her party. As Tanner says, 'The Life Force! I am lost' (CP 390).

The Life Force Triumphant

Thus the stage is set for the final act. Before letting us see how the Life Force claims Tanner, however, Shaw returns to his other plot, that concerning Violet Robinson and Hector Malone. Even this, however, has a bearing on Tanner's situation.

A new character is introduced in the person of Hector's father, an Irish-American millionaire who objects to Violet because of her social situation. He wishes his son's marriage to help someone: 'Let him raise himself socially with my money or raise somebody else: so long as there is a social profit somewhere, I'll regard my expenditure as justified. But there must be a profit for someone. A marriage with you would leave things just where they are' (Act Four CP 394).

However, Violet begins to manage the elder Malone so that when it is revealed that she is already married to his son he is only too anxious to swallow his principles and beg her to persuade the outraged young man to allow him to continue to finance him! Shaw shows in this way that he believes that women rule in matters of sex and marriage, and the whole episode points to the eventual capture of Tanner by Ann. The pointer is given to us when Tanner says, 'And that poor devil is a billionaire! one of the master spirits of the age! Led in a string like a pug dog by the first girl who takes the trouble to despise him! I wonder will it ever come to that with me' (CP 397).

At this point the structure of the play demands a lull and a change of direction, while not entirely getting away from the main theme, and it is supplied by Ann's conversation with Octavius. She uses her usual subterfuge when doing anything she wishes to do, by saying that it is at someone else's direction: 'You know that my mother is determined that I shall marry Jack' (CP 398).

She shows that she is the predatory woman when she tells Tavy: 'Theres no such thing as a willing man when you really go for him' (Act Four CP 399), and when Tanner returns that is what she proceeds to do. Prior to this, however, Tanner has been warned of Ann's intentions in an amusing conversation with Mrs. Whitefield:

MRS. WHITEFIELD (*slyly*): She'd suit you better than Tavy. She'd meet her match in you, Jack. I'd like to see her meet her match.

TANNER: No man is a match for a woman, except with a poker and a pair of hobnailed boots. Not always even then.

ACT FOUR CP 400

Violet leaves for her honeymoon, but not before she has told Jack to get married:

VIOLET: The sooner you get married too, the better. You will be much less misunderstood.

TANNER (*restively*): I quite expect to get married in the course of the afternoon. You all seem to have set your minds on it.

ACT FOUR CP 402

The final making of the kill by Ann is high comedy at its best. Tanner desperately tries to avoid marriage but it is obvious that he has lost. The Life Force has conquered and Jack realises the truth of Ann's observations on Octavius and the poetic temperament:

ANN: The poetic temperament's a very nice temperament, very amiable, very harmless and poetic, I daresay; but it's an old maid's temperament.
TANNER: Barren. The Life Force passes it by.
ANN: If thats what you mean by the Life Force, yes. ACT FOUR CP 403

The trap is set and Tanner falls into it. His desperate attempts to escape are foiled by Ann's witty replies, and he is forced to say, 'Oh, you are witty: at the supreme moment the Life Force endows you with every quality'. When Ann reveals that Tanner was made her guardian in her father's will at her request, he feels hypnotised by her magic, although he still tries to resist. He does so in vain since Ann plays her trump card when the others return, by fainting, but not before saying that she has promised to marry Jack.

A nice music-hall touch is provided when Mendoza drinks the glass of brandy brought to revive Ann, but the play ends on a semi-serious note when Tanner gives notice of the intended wedding. In the course of a delightful speech he says, 'What we have both done this afternoon is to renounce happiness, renounce freedom, renounce tranquillity, above all, renounce the romantic possibilities of an unknown future, for the cares of a household and a family' (CP 405). In the remainder of the speech Tanner the revolutionary tries to assert himself once more, but we are aware that he has lost and life has won. In future he will be controlled by the needs of Ann and her children.

'BACK TO METHUSELAH'

Usually Shaw was clear-sighted in assessing his own work and, writing in the Preface to *Back to Methuselah*, he was critical of his success in putting across the doctrine of Creative Evolution in *Man and Superman*: 'But being then at the height of my invention and comedic talent, I decorated it too brilliantly and lavishly' (CPBS 545). After mentioning that the Hell scene 'was a dream which did not affect the action of the piece' and was detachable from the play, he goes on to say, 'The effect was so vertiginous, apparently, that nobody noticed the new religion in the centre of the intellectual whirlpool' (CPBS 546). He decided to remedy the situation with 'a second legend of Creative Evolution without distractions and embellishments'. He recognised that 'the exuberance of 1901 [had] aged into the garrulity of 1920' and posterity seems to have agreed with his verdict, as *Back to Methuselah* has remained very much a play for the study rather than for the stage.

It is a vast work consisting of five parts, and takes several evenings to act in its entirety in the theatre. On only one occasion has it been performed in full in one day, although in 1969 great interest was aroused when a slightly shortened version of the cycle was produced at the National Theatre by Clifford Williams and Donald MacKechnie. The play deals with what Shaw calls 'the eternal interest of the philosopher's stone which enables men to live for ever' (CPBS 546), and covers a great span of time. Part One takes place in the Garden of Eden and succeeding parts show us the human race evolving through many centuries until the year 31920 is reached. The theme of the play is stated early in Part One when Adam says, 'I do not like myself. I want to be different; to be better; to begin again and again; to shed myself as a snake sheds its skin' (Part One Act One CP 856). The various parts of the play show us many of the same characters recurring in different guises, 'beginning again and again', acting out Nature's purpose, which is, according to Shaw, to reach a state where matter can be dispensed with and pure thought only will remain.

Unfortunately the play is very uneven, as is perhaps inevitable with a work of this length. Although it contains some undeniably fine sections, such as practically the whole of Part One, parts of 'Tragedy of an Elderly Gentleman' and Lilith's final speech which ends the cycle, the general effect is unsatisfying. Too often we are conscious that Shaw is writing speeches, not writing a play. He himself seems conscious of the dangers as he allows characters to refer to the habit of making a speech which seems to be a universal disease, and occasionally he causes characters to hope that they are not boring others. When the arguments are treated seriously boredom is minimal, but Shaw has even more irritating tricks in this play.

In an attempt to give a sense of the dramatic to the writing he often falls into silliness. He allows characters to interject foolishly in order to gain a cheap laugh, and (a habit that he was never able to resist) he delights in giving his characters absurd nicknames such as Iddy Toodles, or names which he thought would amuse, for example, Joseph Popham Bolge Bluebin Barlow, O.M. Too often he is willing to let the philosophical substance of the play be diminished by superficial digs at contemporary English life, or by childish humour, as illustrated by the following:

BURGE-LUBIN (*jocularly*): Well, illustrious Sage- &-Onions, how are your poor sore feet?
CONFUCIUS (*gravely*): I thank you for your kind enquiries. I am well.

PART THREE CP 893

After a while this kind of thing becomes very tiresome.

'The Gospel of the Brothers Barnabas' depends very much for its interest on the reader's realising that contemporary political figures including Lloyd George are portrayed in it. However, those who saw the 1969 National Theatre production will testify that Burge and Lubin are instantly recognisable types to anyone who has ever watched a party political broadcast on television.

At the end of Part One Eve has a very well-written speech in which she speaks of art and artists, saying that it is the creators of all kinds who make life worth living: 'They never want to die, because they are always learning and always creating either things or wisdom, or at least dreaming of them' (Part One Act Two CP 868). It is a point that is taken up by Lilith towards the end of the play. In lines which remind us of other Shavian characters, such as Shotover and Joan, she says: 'I gave the woman the greatest of gifts: curiosity. By that her seed has been saved from my wrath; for I also am curious; and I have waited always to see what they will do tomorrow. Let them feed that appetite well for me. I say, let them dread, of all things, stagnation. . . ' (Part Five CP 962). This could be the motto of the play. 'The pursuit of omnipotence and omniscience' (Part Two CP 886) is seen by Franklyn Barnabas as Nature's aim, and throughout the play Shaw makes it quite clear that mankind can only survive if it is able to justify its existence. He plays with the idea of great longevity, but mainly to show how it brings an increased sense of responsibility to those who possess it. As Zoo says in 'Tragedy of an Elderly Gentleman', 'for to a shortliver increase of years is only increase of sorrow; but to a longliver every extra year is a prospect which forces him to stretch his faculties to the utmost to face it' (Part Four Act One CP 925).

The play's strength lies in the way Shaw is able to throw up ideas on all kinds of subjects, including politics, religion, science and art. Much of the talk in 'Tragedy of an Elderly Gentleman', even in 'The Gospel of the Brothers Barnabas', is provocative and forces us to think again about our preconceptions. As a serious contribution to the discussion of Evolution the play is by no means as stimulating as its Preface, but because of the capacity it shows for rhetoric and wit it deserves to be read, although it has many faults and cannot stand beside *Man and Superman* as a successful stage play.

'THE SIMPLETON OF THE UNEXPECTED ISLES'

In 1934, when he was coming towards the end of his career as a dramatist of note, Shaw wrote *The Simpleton of the Unexpected Isles* in which he once again took up the theme of Creative Evolution. In this play, which makes no attempt to be other than fantastic, Shaw progresses from the view that he appears to hold in parts of 'Don Juan in Hell' and in *Back to Methuselah*, that pure, disembodied thought will be the salvation of the world, to a position in which he advocates a necessity for improvement of life on this earth. The Unexpected Isles are visited by an angel, as the Day of Judgment has been announced. From what he tells the inhabitants and what we hear of events throughout the rest of the world we gather that those who do not work must die, as 'The angels are weeding the garden' (Act Two CP 1245). It is a point of view that Shaw had always held in essence, but we might note in passing that he had recently visited Russia where he had seen a society actually working on this principle.

The play is not very compelling in the theatre, although it created some interest when it was revived in 1966 at the Birmingham Repertory Theatre. It contains too little dramatic conflict, and the only successful creations as characters are the simpleton and the angel (and they are really caricatures). The last scene of the play is completely undramatic and consists largely of reading from newspapers and of one character relaying to others broadcast news received by telephone.

Nevertheless, it is obvious that Shaw was vitally serious in what he was saying in this play, and certain striking phrases and speeches prevent us from dismissing it as uninteresting. He tells us that 'Someday Heaven will get tired of lazy people' (CP 1239), and that 'The lives which have no use, no meaning, no purpose, will fade out. You will have to justify your existence or perish' (CP 1241). We are forced to reconsider our position when the angel's answer to Mrs. Hyering's question 'But where does the end of the world come in?' is 'The Day of Judgment is not the end of the world, but the end of its childhood and the beginning of its responsible maturity' (CP 1241).

In spite of occasional examples of silliness in the newspaper reports read out to the others by Sir Charles, we can see that Shaw means us to take note when Prola says, in one of the last speeches in the play, 'Let men despair and become cynics and pessimists because in the Unexpected Isles all their little plans fail: women will never let go their hold on life. We are not here to fulfil prophecies and fit ourselves into puzzles, but to wrestle with life as it comes. And it never comes as we expect it to come' (CP 1246). Her husband, Pra, sees that he 'must continue to strive for more knowledge and more power' (CP 1247). They realise that they need one another to live, that surprise and wonder are the very breath of being, and routine is death. Every day must be a day of wonder.

We see here Shaw's anxiety to put across the message that recurs in so many of his plays. That message can be summarised as

'Live dangerously. Do not attempt to plan to the exclusion of risk in life. Without risk and work life is not worth living.' *Man and Superman* is the only one of the three plays examined in this chapter to be revived at all frequently in the theatre, and then, as we have already noted, the third act is seldom played. This does not mean, however, that the ordinary theatre-goer remains ignorant of Shaw's doctrine of Creative Evolution.

The skeleton of *Man and Superman* that is left when Act Three is removed still contains sufficient to illustrate Shaw's attitudes towards the function of the sexual relationship which he sees as the basis of all human development. In the play itself he shows Creative Evolution in action, which is surely better than talking about it, as his characters tend to do in the two other plays under discussion. He lets us *see* the pursuit of Tanner by Ann Whitefield, just as he shows us, in the last act of *You Never Can Tell* (written in 1896), Gloria Clandon dominating Valentine, the dentist, and forcing him to marry her. Examples such as these show how effectively ideas can be put across to an audience in dramatic terms.

Some have criticised Shaw's technique in *Man and Superman*, saying that the brilliance of his comedy detracts from his effectiveness as a teacher in the play. To counterbalance this view many would answer that effective teaching can only be achieved if the interest of those being taught is obtained. I would venture to say that the more consciously didactic Shaw was in those plays which deal with Creative Evolution the less effective he was in transmitting his message.

4

The Religious Plays

It is artificial to discuss Shaw's plays under separate headings such as Humour, Religion, Evolution, since there is often an overlap, religion for instance being dealt with partly in terms of humour in *Androcles and the Lion*, but in this chapter it may prove helpful to examine three plays in which Shaw deals primarily with the question of religion, in order to discover what opinions he wishes to communicate and the means he uses to do so.

At the outset it is necessary to point out that Shaw was not a Christian and that his views on religion are probably best gained from those plays dealt with in the chapter on Evolution. Nevertheless, in *Major Barbara*, *Androcles and the Lion* and *Saint Joan*, he is concerned with the subject of religious belief as it affects human conduct, and, as we might expect, he sometimes looks at things from the point of view of a social reformer. He is inclined to believe that before man can spare time to afford the luxury of devoting thought to spiritual matters he must be well fed and decently housed, so that it might be said that Shaw's religion is essentially centred on man. However, the plays do move outside the realm of social criticism and examine the question of belief in a higher power than man organising the universe, and we shall find that Shaw, though not a Christian, was in no way hostile to religious thought. The rather optimistic belief in a Life Force tirelessly working for the best is only given an incidental hearing in these three plays (the three main women characters, Barbara, Lavinia and Joan, can be seen as organising females in direct line of descent from Ann Whitefield) and Shaw concentrates on those factors which go to make up a truly religious person. The answers he comes up with are, not surprisingly, somewhat paradoxical, but show a profound respect on his part for deep religious belief.

'MAJOR BARBARA'

Major Barbara, first produced in 1905, is the earliest of the three plays and in some ways the most puzzling. It is difficult to be certain whether Shaw intends us to assume defeat or victory for Barbara at the end of the play, so that the reader is left with a nagging feeling of dissatisfaction which is perhaps accounted for by Shaw himself not quite having made up his mind about Barbara. There seems to be some lack of consistency in her character after the scene in the Salvation Army shelter, but the impact of the rhetoric in the last act tends to sweep us along when watching or reading the play, so that it is only later that we begin to feel disturbed. In any event few will wish to deny the excellence of the stagecraft and the gripping quality of the material of the play as a whole.

The Preface contains some of Shaw's most trenchant writing and makes it clear that his main aim in the play was to show 'that the greatest of our evils, and the worst of our crimes is poverty, and that our first duty, to which every other consideration should be sacrificed, is not to be poor' (CPBS 118). This is a doctrine he has preached previously in *Mrs. Warren's Profession* and *Widowers' Houses*, but in *Major Barbara* he goes further by actually showing the results of poverty on the stage; we do not just hear about its effects in conversations between comfortably off middle-class people. The play, which has a basically respectful attitude towards the social work being done at that time by the Salvation Army, turns sour in its implicit condemnation of a society that organises itself in such a way as to make such work necessary, and there is no doubt that many of the original audience were offended by what they took to be a condemnation of the Salvation Army. It is true that Shaw gives his devil (Undershaft) the best tunes, but his criticism of the Salvation Army's methods is mild compared with Orwell's criticism of a similar organisation nearly thirty years later in *Down and Out in Paris and London*. Undershaft speaks of '. . . chopping firewood, eating bread and treacle, and being forced to kneel down from time to time to thank heaven for it: knee drill, I think you call it.' He continues, 'It is cheap work converting starving men with a Bible in one hand and a slice of bread in the other. I will undertake to convert West Ham to Mahometanism on the same terms' (CP 499).

Orwell describes tramps in the 'thirties going to a chapel for tea and buns: 'The lady handed out the tea, and while we ate and drank she moved to and fro, talking benignly. She talked upon religious subjects—about Jesus Christ always having a soft spot for poor rough men like us, and about how quickly the time passed when you were in a church, and what a difference it made to a man on the road if he said his prayers regularly.' The captive audience is made to sing a hymn and take part in prayers before departing:

> 'Well,' said somebody as soon as we were out of hearing, 'the trouble's over. I thought them —— prayers was never going to end.'
> 'You 'ad your bun,' said another, 'you got to pay for it.'
> 'Pray for it, you mean. Ah, you don't get much for nothing. They can't even give you a twopenny cup of tea without you go down on your —— knees for it.'   DOWN AND OUT IN PARIS AND LONDON

At least the Secularist Peter Shirley was not made to do that at Barbara's shelter.

The play begins with all the appearances of a social comedy, and Act One is set in 'the library in Lady Britomart Undershaft's house in Wilton Crescent (CP 460). We are at once in the world of an Oscar Wilde comedy where incomes of £2,000 a year (a huge sum in 1905) are looked on as normal, a fact that throws into relief the poverty that Shaw shows us at the Salvation Army shelter later in the play. The exposition scene between Lady Britomart (a typical organising matron, rather like a more formidable Mrs. Higgins) and her son, Stephen, is most skilfully managed. We are given all essential information concerning the strange family situation of the Undershafts in a way that is always amusing. We are never conscious that we are having facts loaded on to us because Shaw makes his two characters so instantly real. They may be types rather than individuals, but perhaps the defence of this would be that so many people of any class, even today, react in a way that is literally 'true to type'. In a later scene, at the beginning of Act Three, Shaw, speaking through Undershaft, mercilessly mocks the Stephens of this world with their assumptions based on class attitudes and upbringing, rather than on a clear-sighted examination of the facts.

The main points that emerge from the opening section of the play are that Lady Britomart's estranged husband, Andrew Undershaft, is a fabulously wealthy manufacturer of armaments and that Lady Britomart's daughter, Barbara, has joined the Salvation Army, discharged her maid, and is living on a pound a week. Lady Britomart explains that Undershaft is a foundling and reveals that one of the reasons she separated from him was his insistence on adhering to the tradition that the Undershaft business should descend to another foundling, which would cut out Stephen from the inheritance. In addition she prepares us for Undershaft's unhypocritical cast of mind when she says, 'But your father didnt exactly *do* wrong things: he said them and thought them: that was what was so dreadful. He really had a sort of religion of wrongness. . . . I couldnt forgive Andrew for preaching immorality while he practised morality' (CP 463).

Barbara, we are told, is engaged to an Australian-born professor of Greek, Adolphus Cusins, 'whom she has picked up in the street, and who pretends to be a Salvationist, and actually plays the big drum for her in public because he has fallen head over ears in love with her' (CP 461). Lady Britomart sees it as Undershaft's duty to provide for his family now that they are of marriageable age. Stephen is quite against the idea and Shaw shows us just how impractical he is when he says, 'We cannot take money from him. I had rather go and live in some cheap place like Bedford Square or even Hampstead than take a farthing of his money' (CP 463). After Lady Britomart has completely overridden Stephen's objections to asking Undershaft to visit the house Shaw ends this section of the play with an amusing piece of theatricality: 'Thank you, Stephen: I knew you would give me the right advice when it was properly explained to you. I have asked your father to come this evening' (CP 464).

We learn quite a lot about Barbara before we see her. Lady Britomart's lack of advance warning of Undershaft's visit is explained by the fact that it will not allow Barbara, who, 'Ever since they made her a major in the Salvation Army ... has developed a propensity to have her own way and order people about' (CP 464), to refuse to meet her father or make a fuss. Not surprisingly therefore the play develops into a contest between Barbara and her father, the one on the side of God, the other very much echoing Shaw's view that salvation must come to us solely because of our own efforts.

The crux of the play is the confrontation of viewpoints that they represent, and the plot revolves round the bargain made between father and daughter in Act One:

UNDERSHAFT: Well, I will make a bargain with you. If I go to see you tomorrow in your Salvation Shelter, will you come the day after to see me in my cannon works?

BARBARA: Take care. It may end in your giving up the cannons for the sake of the Salvation Army.

UNDERSHAFT: Are you sure it will not end in your giving up the Salvation Army for the sake of the cannons? CP 469

In view of later developments we should also take note of a significant error in recognition on Undershaft's part when he is being introduced to his family and their prospective marriage partners. After mistaking Charles Lomax for his son Stephen, and having the mistake pointed out to him, Undershaft passes on to the professor, Cusins, saying 'Then *you* must be my son' (CP 467). The sentence can be taken in two ways and foreshadows exactly what does happen at the end of the play when Cusins becomes the heir to the armaments business, having established a rather tenuous claim to being a foundling.

Act One contains a good deal of serious material that will be enlarged on later by Shaw, but we should be doing him a disservice if we failed to observe how cleverly he uses his sense of comedy to keep the audience's attention in this section of the play. The 'silly ass' character of Charles Lomax is extremely amusing, as is the way in which he is so tartly put down by Lady

Britomart. For example, when it is learned that Undershaft is coming to the house, Sarah says, 'Well, he cant eat us, I suppose. *I* dont mind'; to be followed by

LOMAX (*chuckling*): I wonder how the old man will take it.
LADY BRITOMART: Much as the old woman will, no doubt, Charles.
LOMAX (*abashed*): I didnt mean—at least—
LADY BRITOMART: You didnt *think*, Charles. You never do; and the result is, you never mean anything. ACT ONE CP 465–6

This is only one of the occasions on which Lomax speaks out without considering the effect of what he is about to say. Generally the result is to cause a laugh and to give the audience a safety valve when they are in danger of being overwhelmed by so many ideas. With Lomax on stage the play is in no danger of becoming over-solemn.

In spite of the interest of the first act with all its variety, the scenes at the shelter and at Perivale St. Andrews are those which contain the core of the play. In them we find Shaw trying to work out what constitutes true religion, and how it should affect our lives.

The scenes make their impact largely because of the contrast between their settings. The Salvation Army shelter, without being sordid, is a depressing place, exuding an air of poverty, while Shaw stresses the grace and beauty of Undershaft's town and foundry.

Incidentally we should note the sharp social criticism contained in Shaw's stage directions at the beginning of Act Two, with the emphasis on poverty's power to age working-class women, and the uselessness of the idle rich.

The Shelter Scene

It is in Act Two that we see 'Major' Barbara, the selfless, efficient organiser of her shelter, and we are left in no doubt as to her great abilities. In the midst of poverty, faced with difficult customers of different kinds in Peter Shirley and Bill Walker, she is always in control—at least until the end of the act. Her sympathy and human warmth are shown in her dealings with Peter

71

Shirley, and the first hint in the play of Shaw's attitude to belief comes out in one of her remarks to him. After she has guessed that he is not a Christian, Barbara says: 'My own father's a Secularist, I think. Our Father—yours and mine—fulfils himself in many ways; and I daresay he knew what he was about when he made a Secularist of you' (CP 474). The implication that true religion is to be found in an attitude sincerely held, however unorthodox it may be, is something that Shaw is to return to in the play and also in *Androcles and the Lion*, as we shall see later.

Barbara is seen as a formidable creature in her encounter with Bill Walker, the tough who comes to the shelter to take away his girl, Mog Habbijam, who has been there for help. He terrorises the weaker 'soupkitcheners', as he calls them, and strikes the young Salvation Army girl, Jenny Hill. It is noticeable, however, that Peter Shirley stands up to him, but perhaps rather too much of a coincidence in view of what happens to Bill later that the brother of Shirley's son-in-law should be the celebrated Todger Fairmile—'Him that won £20 off the Japanese wrastler at the music hall by standing out 17 minutes 4 seconds agen him' (CP 473). However, although soon afterwards Bill is physically humiliated by Todger, who is now a sergeant in the Salvation Army, it is the way that Barbara works on his conscience that makes the greatest impression on him and on us.

He has been somewhat put down by Shirley's information that 'the major here is the Earl o Stevenage's granddaughter' (CP 473), and when Barbara enters, 'Bill, cowed, sits down in the corner on a form, and turns his back on them' (CP 474). When Barbara speaks to him she does so unemotionally and briskly, putting his name down in her book and entering him 'as the man who—struck—poor Little Jenny Hill—in the mouth'. By insisting quietly on his brutality Barbara reduces Bill to a state of guilt, and to his alarm speaks of saving his soul. She will not leave him alone, so that he goes off to Canning Town in order to repay Jenny for having hit her. His sense of rough justice tells him that if Todger Fairmile hits him it will make matters square. Adolphus agrees with him, but Barbara chips in with 'Two black eyes wont make one white one, Bill' (CP 477). Throughout the scene it is amusing

A wood engraving by John Farleigh for *The Black Girl in Search of God*.
The figure jumping the gate is a portrait of Shaw.

Shaw at the Malvern Festival, 1932. The group includes J. T. Grein (first on the left of the bottom row) and Sir Barry Jackson (at the right end of the bottom row).

A scene from the first London Production of *Heartbreak House*, 1921.

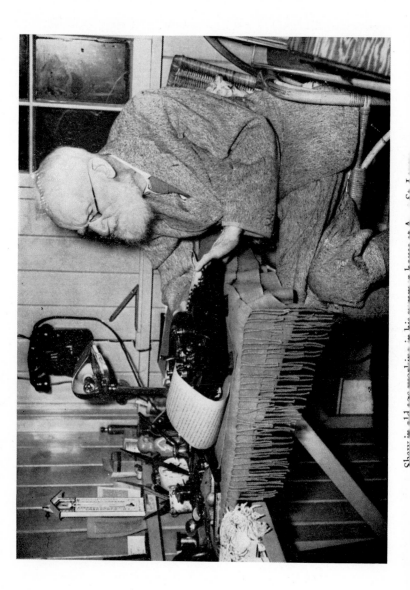

Shown is old-age pensioner in his own room at home at Ashton-under-Lyne

to note how horrified Bill is by Barbara's preaching at him. We see this when Barbara introduces him to Adolphus:

BARBARA: Oh! there you are, Dolly. Let me introduce a new friend of mine, Mr. Bill Walker. This is my bloke, Bill: Mr. Cusins. (*Cusins salutes with his drumstick*)

BILL: Gowin to merry im?

BARBARA: Yes.

BILL (*fervently*): Gawd elp im! Gaw-aw-aw-awd elp im!

BARBARA: Why? Do you think he wont be happy with me?

BILL: Awve aony ed to stend it for a mawnin: e'll ev to stend it for a lawftawm.   ACT TWO CP 477

Just before Bill goes off to Canning Town, Undershaft arrives. We have already been given vivid examples of the evil effects of poverty, which has been shown to cause hypocrisy, lying and loss of self-respect; now Shaw brings his spokesman back on to the scene. Immediately the theme of the play is restated for us when Undershaft tells Barbara that *his* religion is being a millionaire.

The antithetical exchange between Shirley and Undershaft leaves us in no doubt as to the point Shaw was trying to put over. Barbara has just said 'Youre not a Millionaire, are you, Peter?'

SHIRLEY: No: and proud of it.

UNDERSHAFT (*gravely*): Poverty, my friend, is not a thing to be proud of.

SHIRLEY (*angrily*): Who made your millions for you? Me and my like. Whats kep us poor? Keepin you rich. I wouldnt have your conscience, not for all your income.

UNDERSHAFT: I wouldnt have your income not for all your conscience, Mr. Shirley.   ACT TWO CP 476

The remainder of the act is taken up by a conversation between Adolphus and Undershaft, the return of Bill Walker, humiliated, from Canning Town, and Mrs. Baines's attempts to get enough money to keep the Salvation Army shelters open through the hard winter. Barbara, although not on stage the whole time, acts as a link between the episodes, as her influence is great on all the parties concerned.

We have noticed that Undershaft and Cusins did not have a

great deal to say to one another in Act One, but now they make up for it. Cusins is immediately taken by Undershaft's honesty when he says that the only two things necessary for salvation are money and gunpowder. The short section following this revelation is of great interest since it expresses Shaw's opinions, though not in literal terms:

CUSINS: Excuse me: is there any place in your religion for honor, justice, truth, love, mercy and so forth?
UNDERSHAFT: Yes: they are the graces and luxuries of a rich, strong, and safe life.
CUSINS: Suppose one is forced to choose between them and money or gunpowder?
UNDERSHAFT: Choose money and gunpowder; for without enough of both you cannot afford the others.   ACT TWO CP 478

We should not suppose that Shaw advocated violence and revolution. He was himself the least bloodthirsty of men, but here he is surely saying, in a metaphorical way, that one must fight for one's rights and that without the preliminary skirmishing nothing will be achieved in the way of social equality. Undershaft reinforces this view by insisting on the necessity of acquiring 'money enough for a decent life, and power enough to be your own master' (CP 478).

Beneath the debate between Undershaft and Cusins it is obvious that the two men feel a strong attraction towards one another, so that we are not surprised to find Adolphus marching away with Undershaft at the end of the act, and later in the play taking over the cannon business from him. Cusins prepares us for this when he admits to being 'a sort of collector of religions', and although he claims to be a sincere Salvationist it is obvious that he is drawn towards the rather devilish power of Undershaft. He recognises in him a man who lives according to truth as he sees it, and does not direct his actions according to outmoded social conventions. Cusins himself admits that what fascinates him about the Salvation Army are its qualities 'of joy, of love, of courage: it has banished the fear and remorse and despair of the old hell-ridden evangelical sects: it marches to fight the devil with trumpet and

74

drum, with music and dancing, with banner and palm, as becomes a sally from heaven by its happy garrison'. We are not surprised by his reply, when Undershaft charges him with readiness to convert the Salvation Army to the worship of Dionysos:

CUSINS: The business of the Salvation Army is to save, not to wrangle about the name of the pathfinder. Dionysos or another: what does it matter?   ACT TWO CP 479

After this speech, we know that we can expect Cusins to seek his salvation in his own way, and we can gather that he will have Shaw's approval, just as Peter Shirley has his approval for being a Secularist, and Ferrovius, in *Androcles and the Lion*, has his approval for staying true to his real self and killing the gladiators in the arena, even though the act conflicts with what is usually expected of a Christian.

The interchange between Cusins and Undershaft reveals that the millionaire intends Barbara to carry on with his gospel of 'money and gunpowder. Freedom and power. Command of life and command of death' (CP 479). In a splendidly effective quiet speech he underlines the fact that poverty is hateful and says that to love poverty, disease and suffering is wicked: 'We three must stand together above the common people: how else can we help their children to climb up beside us? Barbara must belong to us, not to the Salvation Army' (CP 480). This section of the play ends with a hint of what is to come when Undershaft speaks of buying the Salvation Army, and there is a display of verbal fireworks in a rapid exchange of views about what the Army does for the poor, Undershaft capping every statement of Cusins's with a cynical, practical reason for welcoming every reform Cusins mentions.

When Barbara returns to the yard from her evangelical meeting in Cripps Lane, Shaw prepares us in some measure for the disillusionment that is to be hers at the end of the act by showing how easily she is taken in by Snobby Price whose false confession has moved the crowd so much that they have contributed four and tenpence to the collection. She refuses her father's ironic offer of twopence as 'the millionaire's mite', on the grounds that his money is tainted, so that his eventual agreement to give Mrs. Baines £5,000 obviously causes her immense suffering. However, before this happens, Shaw brings Bill Walker back on the scene.

Bill reveals that he has been used as a carpet by Todger Fairmile, who has led prayers for his salvation, and we see how his feelings of guilt for having struck Jenny Hill are still preying on him. He wishes to discharge his debt with money, which immediately reminds us of Barbara's words to her father when refusing his offer—'You cant buy your salvation here for twopence: you must work it out' (CP 481). Nevertheless, Bill throws a sovereign down on the upturned bass drum, hoping to gain some peace by so doing. Barbara still maintains that the Army is not to be bought and that nothing less than Bill's soul will suffice: 'Youll never have another quiet moment, Bill, until you come round to us. You cant stand out against your salvation' (CP 482). We have the feeling that Barbara is very close to gaining an unwilling convert.

Before the climactic event of Undershaft offering to equal Bodger the brewer's gift of £5,000 to keep the Salvation Army shelters open all winter, there are two other points to notice. Firstly, we should take note of Undershaft's approval of the methods of the poor who rioted in 1886, thus drawing attention to their plight in a way that caused the rich to notice them in a practical fashion to the tune of £49,000 in a single day: this is what Undershaft means by 'money and gunpowder'. Secondly, we have a further indication of Snobby Price's cunning when he steals Bill Walker's sovereign before skulking off to avoid the mother whom he has maligned in his 'confession'.

These are, however, unimportant matters compared to the shock that Barbara experiences when Mrs. Baines accepts Undershaft's help. After her enquiry as to the source of the money offered by a brewer to keep the shelters open, Barbara is silent for some minutes, listening in horror to Mrs. Baines work on Undershaft for the other £5,000 necessary. As the cheque is signed Bill Walker asks pertinently 'Wot prawce selvytion nah?' (CP 484) and Barbara realises that she must speak out.

The ending of the scene is rather complex. Undershaft makes no attempt to disguise from Mrs. Baines the fact that his own fortune depends on bloodshed and slaughter, and yet she is able, through simple faith, to say, 'The longer I live the more proof I see that there is an Infinite Goodness that turns everything to the work of salvation sooner or later'. Barbara is not able to adopt this attitude, particularly when Adolphus appears to desert her as well. He, it seems, is completely captivated by the dynamic qualities of Undershaft that he has recognised earlier in the scene and is, like a follower of Dionysos, temporarily possessed. Barbara is so dispirited by the fact that her father has shown it is possible to buy the Army that she feels that she cannot go to the big meeting and that she may never pray again. As the procession goes off she is led to say, 'Drunkenness and Murder! My God: why hast thou forsaken me?' (CP 485)—a deliberate echo of Christ's words on the cross that was to provoke the charge of blasphemy at the time of the play's first production.

Act Two ends with Barbara very near defeat. She is forced to face the fact that Snobby Price is a fraud and that she has lost the chance of converting Bill Walker, as he has seen that money can seem of greater value than souls. It is not surprising that when we next see her she has discarded her Salvation Army uniform.

The third act begins in Wilton Crescent before the characters go to visit Undershaft's model town and factory. The early part of the scene in the library is amusing, showing Adolphus with a slight hangover—the result of an evening's drinking with Undershaft after the meeting they had both attended. We are also diverted by the exchanges between Charles Lomax and Lady Britomart. Before the departure for Perivale St. Andrews we are once more reminded of the conditions of the Undershaft inheritance since Lady Britomart is adamant that Stephen should be given the opportunity to run the factory. The interchange between Undershaft and his wife gives Shaw an opportunity to snipe at the English educational system and, most important of all from the point of view of the plot, Undershaft tells Lady

Britomart, 'If you want to keep the foundry in the family, you had better find an eligible foundling and marry him to Barbara' (Act Three CP 489).

Stephen

Stephen is a very wooden figure who is only in the play for the requirements of the plot. He has no real individuality and his function is to be on the receiving end of Undershaft's wit or to be the object of Lady Britomart's manoeuvrings. However, the role provides the actor with a great opportunity in the early part of Act Three when he occupies the centre of the stage while discussing his future with his father. His pomposity and the way in which he is convinced he is right on all occasions cause us, in a way, to admire his courage even though we cannot share his opinions. The scene shows him standing up to Undershaft and in the course of their conversation Shaw is able to point out what great prejudices existed in England at the time the play was written and how a conviction of being born to rule, held by those in high places, often masked incompetence. In some of Undershaft's speeches in this section of the play we can see a favourite technique of Shaw's at work: a speech by one character seems to be addressed to another character, but is in reality being directed at the audience. This is particularly true of the speech in which Undershaft tells Stephen that the financiers, not the politicians, govern the country.

Just before the departure of the party to see the factory, Undershaft is forced to see how hard Barbara has been hit by losing Bill Walker's soul the day before when the Salvationists accepted money gained from the armaments business. Undershaft, however, speaks the truth when he tells her that she should not despair as Walker must still bear the mark if he was struck to the heart. This section of the play ends on a note of qualified optimism when Barbara says to her father, 'You may be a devil; but God speaks through you sometimes', and even though she admits that her spirit is troubled, she is ready to visit the 'factory of death', saying that 'There must be some truth or other behind all this frightful irony' (CP 492).

The question that troubles many people reading the last section of the play is whether Shaw shows Barbara convinced of the truth behind the irony in a way that is satisfactory, knowing what we do of her. There can be no doubt, however, that the scene at Perivale St. Andrews contains some of Shaw's finest rhetoric and displays his dramatic sense at its best.

Before the party left Wilton Crescent the audience had been prepared in some measure for the town by Undershaft's sardonic speeches about its facilities for worship and its class structure. The stage direction describing it stresses its idyllic aspect, and Cusins's first remark reinforces this impression: 'Everything perfect! wonderful! real! It only needs a cathedral to be a heavenly city instead of a hellish one' (CP 493). But it is the hellishness of it that is brought home to us early in this scene, when we learn that the new aerial battleship wiped out a fort containing three hundred soldiers at its first trial. The scene contains a great deal of variety, mixing the rhetoric of Undershaft, Cusins and Barbara with the comedy of Stephen, Charles Lomax and Lady Britomart. For instance, it is amusing to see Lomax being led away from the high explosives shed for having dropped a red-hot match in it and to hear him tell the foreman, 'A little bit of British pluck is what *you* want, old chap' (CP 494); while all the acquisitiveness of the British aristocracy comes out in Lady Britomart when she sees the Undershaft possessions: 'They belong to *me*: they are not a man's business. I wont give them up. You must be out of your senses to throw them all away; and if you persist in such folly, I will call in a doctor' (CP 495).

However, Undershaft has reminded her of the tradition of the inheritance, and the chief dramatic action of this scene concerns its disposal. Lady Britomart, anxious for Barbara's future, suggests that Adolphus should inherit, as Stephen is too perverse to be fit for the position. It appears that Adolphus can get round the difficulty of not really being a foundling, as his parents' marriage, though legal in Australia, is not in England, since his mother is his father's deceased wife's sister. A fine battle ensues between Undershaft and Cusins over terms, in which Cusins once more seems overtaken with Dionysiac power, as he was at the end of the shelter scene. He manipulates Undershaft and forces a hard bargain with him, but Barbara will not be drawn into the negotiations. In fact we sense that she is suffering even more deeply than before when she asks Cusins, 'Is the bargain closed, Dolly? Does your soul belong to him now?' (CP 497).

Cusins's reply is that 'The real tug of war is yet to come' and he and Undershaft now proceed to discuss the moral question.

In the course of the following speeches the close link between Barbara and her father is stressed. It is evident that Shaw intends us to see Undershaft as a divine instrument, just as Barbara is motivated by her love of God, although her faith has suffered a setback because the power of the distillers and armaments manufacturers has been shown to her. Undershaft says enigmatically that the factory is driven by a will of which he is a part, and in several fine speeches returns to the theme of Shaw's Preface—that poverty is a crime. He speaks of the seven deadly sins: 'Food, clothing, firing, rent, taxes, respectability, and children. Nothing can lift those seven millstones from Man's neck but money; and the spirit cannot soar until the millstones are lifted' (CP 498). We can see a pointer to the way in which things will go later in the play when he challenges Barbara to try to convert his men, whose souls are hungry because their bodies are full. All of Shaw's power of rhetoric is to be found in these speeches in which Undershaft condemns the demoralising nature of poverty, and the writer is even sufficiently confident to draw attention to the fact that he is sermonising, by allowing Lady Britomart to interject 'Stop making speeches, Andrew. This is not the place for them' (CP 499). In one sense we agree, but the vigour of those speeches can captivate any audience.

Undershaft upsets Lady Britomart when he tells Adolphus that society can only be changed by those who hold the power of life and death, but, significantly, Barbara is not ready to be led away from her father, saying that running away from wicked people does not save them. It is obvious that she is at a critical point spiritually and Shaw leads up to a conversation between Cusins and her that is of great importance to both of them. Undershaft requires a decision from Adolphus as to whether he will take over the business and Cusins is worried in case Barbara will not marry him if he makes the wrong choice. Undershaft and the others leave Barbara and Adophus alone for a while and Adolphus makes it clear that he is going to accept the offer.

To some extent his choice is influenced by Undershaft's statement that 'society cannot be saved until either the Professors of Greek take to making gunpowder, or else the makers of gunpowder become Professors of Greek' (CP 500). For in Adolphus two strains, those of power and poetry, are united, as Eric Bentley noted when he wrote of Cusins combining the idealism of Barbara with the realism of her father. Even so I feel that we must agree with those who find the end of the play rather unsatisfactory; Cusins lacks the magnetism of Undershaft and Barbara's regaining of her faith is less convincing than her previous disillusionment. Nevertheless, the interchange between Barbara and Cusins produces some striking writing and shows that both of them have developed in a way that leaves them ready to face the challenge of life. Cusins is determined to use his newly gained power to make war on war and Barbara has realised that she must look for her work of salvation everywhere. 'Turning our backs on Bodger and Undershaft is turning our backs on life', she says, and her next speech shows that she has made an advance in her thinking: 'There is no wicked side: life is all one. And I never wanted to shirk my share in whatever evil must be endured, whether it be sin or suffering' (CP 502). Certainly the shelter scene showed her to be ready to share in the suffering, but we were not convinced then that she was entirely without a certain priggishness. To some extent even now we feel slightly uneasy, but perhaps this is because Shaw has made her pain so real at the end of Act Two that we cannot readily be reassured of her recovery of faith in her own powers.

The play ends on a rising note with the themes of religion and social reform closely connected once again. Barbara indicates that people are put on the earth to be useful and she recognises that her father was right when he challenged her to try to save

Fs

his well-fed workers: 'I have got rid of the bribe of bread. I have got rid of the bribe of heaven. Let God's work be done for its own sake: the work he had to create us to do because it cannot be done except by living men and women.' She tells Cusins that her courage has come back and that 'Major Barbara will die with the colors' (CP 503). Certainly her task will not be easy but she appears to be approaching it with ecstatic enthusiasm. Yet it should be noticed that the 'devil's disciple' of the play, Undershaft, has the last word, which is perhaps a reminder on Shaw's part that he is still in control, that until the visionaries (or Professors of Greek) are ready to soil their hands with practical matters, the world will be controlled by those who resist their benevolent impulses, or have never had any, and concentrate sternly on worldly affairs.

'ANDROCLES AND THE LION'

Seven years after the production of *Major Barbara*, Shaw turned once again to religion as the subject for a play, and he wrote *Androcles and the Lion*, 'as a sample of what children like in contrast to Barrie's *Peter Pan* which seemed to me a sample of what adults think children like'. As we might expect from this comment, the play contains a great deal that appeals to children, but it would be a mistake to regard it as a children's play.

Androcles and the Lion is quite short, consisting of a prologue and two acts. The prologue and the latter part of the second act serve as a humorous framework to the serious discussion of the play, dealing as they do with the confrontations of Androcles and his lion. Even in the prologue, however, Shaw never lets us forget that the reason for Androcles and his wife being on the move so that they have to face wild beasts in the forest is that the followers of the Christian religion are being persecuted by the Romans. From the outset, therefore, the theme of the play is put before us and we are forced to consider why men will undergo deprivation and torture for their beliefs.

Anachronisms

Shaw has taken an old story and adapted it for his purposes, making Androcles a Christian. As we shall see, he takes many liberties with historical accuracy in this play and a great deal of his humour comes from the use of deliberate anachronisms. For instance, as he himself pointed out in a programme note when the play was first produced, the Roman centurion and the Roman captain act exactly as we would expect a British sergeant and a British company officer to do, and, with complete disregard for chronology, he allows his Christians to sing 'Onward Christian Soldiers', an English hymn of the 19th century. However, some of the most striking examples of humour in this vein are connected with Androcles' wife, Megaera, a character who disappears from the play after the Prologue.

The events of the Prologue remind us of pantomime. After the opening sequence in which the wounded lion has endeavoured unsuccessfully to remove the thorn from his forepaw and retired to sleep, Androcles and Megaera come on the scene. Immediately we are in a readily recognised world—that of the comic picture postcard in which large wives dominate puny working-class husbands. It is a stock relationship that has always been found funny by readers and audiences, as we can see by examining the portrayal of Noah's wife in the medieval mystery plays and then comparing it with certain popular television series in our own day. In the course of their conversation it emerges that Androcles is a Christian while his wife is not and that they have had to leave their home to avoid persecution. Shaw makes the important point that the early Christians were regarded as 'dirty disreputable blaspheming atheists' by many, including Megaera.

The Prologue contains a great deal to amuse. Androcles is presented as stoically putting up with his wife's tirades and yet scoring off her in a quiet way. When Megaera complains that he spent hours talking to the stray animals he brought home when he hadn't a word for her we sympathise with Androcles' reply, 'They never answered back, darling' (Prologue CP 685).

There is no attempt on Shaw's part to portray Megaera and Androcles as historically credible people and it is amusing to hear her say, in the manner of a 20th-century barmaid, 'My father owned his own public-house; and sorrowful was the day for me when you first came drinking in our bar' (CP 685).

After the argument between the two the scene proceeds with an episode of delightful humour followed by a piece of slapstick fantasy. Megaera, irritated beyond endurance by Androcles' behaviour, decides to leave him, but almost trips over the sleeping lion. Shaw skilfully manages to combine humour with an indication of Androcles' bravery at this point when he makes him say, 'Meggy: theres one chance for you. Itll take him pretty nigh twenty minutes to eat me (I'm rather stringy and tough) and you can escape in less time than that' (CP 686). However, Megaera faints and Androcles is left to face the lion.

Although he is afraid, Androcles is resolute, but as soon as he sees that the lion is injured his manner changes to one of compassion. In a very funny speech he speaks to the lion in baby talk: 'Has it made um too sick to eat a nice little Christian man for um's breakfast? Oh, a nice little Christian man will get um's thorn out for um; and then um shall eat the nice Christian man and the nice Christian man's nice big tender wifey pifey' (CP 686). Reaction to this speech in the theatre always confirms that this is, as Shaw claimed, 'a sample of what children like'.

The scene ends on a note of gaiety with Androcles and the lion waltzing away into the jungle, while the recovered Megaera paradoxically reviles her husband by calling him a coward for dancing with a lion when he hasn't danced with her for years. The stage is set for the important business of the play, a consideration of Christian belief as held by Lavinia, Spintho, Ferrovius and Androcles, but the time spent on the Prologue has not been wasted. Obviously, in view of the play's ending, Shaw had to show how Androcles and his lion became acquainted, but we have also absorbed the play's climate, one in which persecution of Christians is the normal, accepted thing. The remainder of the play concerns the effects of persecution on the Christian characters.

In Act One we are shown the gathering together of Christian prisoners who are to perish in the arena if they refuse to sacrifice to the Roman gods, while Act Two deals with events on the actual day of the gladiatorial combat. Perhaps because of the shortness of the play characters are not drawn in any great depth, but Shaw's skill in making them sufficiently interesting to hold our attention is obvious. Lavinia and the Captain can be said to play the 'straight' parts, while Spintho and Ferrovius (the man of iron) provide comic sidelights, although in vastly differing ways.

Lavinia and the Captain

Lavinia and the Captain are not particularly interesting as characters, although we should note that Lavinia is another example of Shaw's strong women, as we see when she makes short work of the patrician Lentulus when he tries to flirt with her. However, the main point of the exchanges between Lavinia and the Captain is to emphasise the qualities that a truly religious person must have. The Captain does not enjoy leading his prisoners to execution, but, as a reasonable man to whom the religious temperament is completely foreign, he fails to see why people should be willing to die for their faith. We feel that he is made uneasy, however, when Lavinia tells him that her faith, like his sword, needs testing, and he attempts to draw their conversation to a close. Later in the scene Lavinia shows what her faith means to her when she says, 'Religion is such a great thing that when I meet really religious people we are friends at once, no matter what name we give to the divine will that made us and moves us' (Act One CP 689). She goes on to say that her objection to the Roman gods is that they are worshipped by people who do not know the meaning of religion and who look on them as symbols of terror and darkness, cruelty and greed.

Spintho and Ferrovius

Other examples of Christian faith are put before us in the persons of Spintho and Ferrovius. Spintho is a despicable example of one who has lived a life of sin which he does not really regret and who hopes to achieve salvation by being martyred as a Christian. As we can see from reading Shaw's Preface to the play, this is not a truly Christian attitude, as Jesus laid emphasis upon true repentance and reformation of character. Few can be sorry when Spintho's nerve fails him in Act Two and he runs away to burn the incense, only to be eaten by the lion. Before that, however, he has been a central figure in an amusing scene with Ferrovius when he dares to imply that animals do not go to heaven when they die.

Ferrovius plays an important part in the play by reverting to his true beliefs and killing the gladiators in the arena, thus gaining the release of all the Christian prisoners except Androcles. Before that happens, he is the cause of much amusement in Act One. As his name implies he is a giant of a man, and he is exceedingly naïve. He fails to see that his success in making converts is the result of his great size and it is delightful to hear him when he tells Lentulus, who has tried to humiliate him, 'I have not always been faithful. The first man who struck me as you have just struck me was a stronger man than you: he hit me harder than I expected. I was tempted and fell; and it was then that I first tasted bitter shame. I never had a happy moment after that until I had knelt and asked his forgiveness by his bedside in the hospital' (CP 691). We learn from Androcles that Ferrovius is afraid that he might resist the gladiators at the last moment and it is no surprise to hear Lavinia say that that would be splendid.

The final act of the play combines humour and horror. Once again Shaw attempts to make us see things through 20th-century eyes and we are shown events at the arena as though we were backstage in a modern theatre. There is a call boy, and the gladiators behave like temperamental actors, even brushing their hair and looking at themselves in mirrors before they go out to fight. Nevertheless, in spite of all this, there is no attempt to gloss over the fact that the Christians are going to die.

The emperor is chiefly a figure of fun, particularly in his encounter with Androcles, who is recognised by the lion as its friend who took the thorn from its paw. Shaw shows masterly control of his medium here, taking us back to the atmosphere of the Prologue. We accept the lion both as a lion and as a pantomime animal, and the slapstick atmosphere generated helps to end the play on a happy note. Yet, even so, we are not allowed to forget that the tyrannical Romans would have had Ferrovius, Androcles and the other Christians put to death for their beliefs if it had not been for Ferrovius' bravery in the arena and the lucky chance which brought Androcles and the lion together again.

Religion must be Positive

There can be few people who would claim that the play has the stature of *Major Barbara*, and yet it is important for the light it casts on Shaw's attitude towards religion. The very long Preface to the play deals in stimulating fashion with Shaw's thoughts on the gospels, but we can obtain some idea of his beliefs from an examination of the conduct of Lavinia, Androcles, Spintho and Ferrovius in the play itself. Those who show a positive attitude are rewarded, even though their conduct may not be specifically Christian. Ferrovius, for instance, acts according to his nature and decides that he 'must serve the gods that are, not the God that will be' (Act Two CP 702). To some extent he reminds us of Undershaft in *Major Barbara*, in that in both men Shaw seems to be approving of any positive belief so long as it is strongly held. It may not be an orthodox way to assess conduct, but then, as Shaw points out in his comments on Christ in the Preface, vigorous leadership, not meek acceptance of direction, can be considered the clue to Christ's magnetic influence on his followers.

Androcles and the Lion has something in it for everyone. It appeals to children (and adults) for its pantomime sequences, it has strongly differentiated characters who are sufficiently deeply drawn for Shaw's purposes and the variety of its language cannot escape any reader. It is not surprising that the play has been regularly revived professionally in recent years, and it has long been a favourite of school dramatic societies.

'SAINT JOAN'

The final play to be dealt with in this chapter on Shaw's religious plays is *Saint Joan*. It was written in the period immediately following Joan's canonisation by the Catholic Church in 1920 and was first produced in Great Britain in 1924. Although it may not be the most frequently performed of Shaw's plays it has always been extremely popular with actresses seeking a vehicle for their talents, and there have been many famous Joans since

Sybil Thorndike, the creator of the part in England. *Saint Joan* is a play that is often liked by those who say that they do not care for Shaw's work in general. It is easy to see why; it has a sincerity and sense of tragedy that are not to be found in some of the other plays, and although Shaw is eager to put across an intellectual message he is not over-anxious to do so. We feel that the character of Joan moved him and that he wrote from the heart about her, so that whereas in certain other plays we are conscious of manipulation of character and events to prove a point, here we feel that Joan is left to make her effect through her goodness and simplicity. Obviously the play is much more complex than the foregoing would seem to suggest, but the fact remains that many who otherwise steer clear of Shaw admit to an admiration for *Saint Joan*.

The play sticks mainly to recorded historical fact, although Shaw obviously has to compress incidents and rearrange material in order to achieve dramatic effects. It is a chronicle play in six scenes together with a controversial epilogue which will demand discussion later. As in *Major Barbara* and *Androcles and the Lion*, the most important woman character is a rebel against the values of most of those who surround her, and is thus a kind of outsider figure, by a consideration of whose actions we are led to judge the actions and motives of the other more conventional characters in the play.

In *Saint Joan* Shaw is concerned, as he was in the two plays discussed earlier in this chapter, with the question of Christian belief and its effect upon those who believe. He is primarily interested in showing the differences between Joan's idea of Christianity and that of the Church, and he makes the point in his Preface that, given the situation at the time in which Joan lived, the Church had no option but to deliver her up for burning as a heretic since she would not do as the Church told her. The alternative was to allow her unprecedented religious freedom and, in spite of all she had done to free her country from England's invasion, this was unthinkable.

In chronicling Joan's life from the time when she took up arms until her execution, Shaw typically introduces a great deal of discussion, with particular regard to the religious attitudes of Joan's day and to the growing concept of nationalism. It is in the course of these sections of the play (such as the conversation between Warwick and Cauchon in Scene Four and the Inquisitor's long speech in Scene Six) that Shaw deliberately makes use of anachronisms, but he explains his reasons for doing so in the Preface to the play. There he writes: 'But it is the business of the stage to make its figures more intelligible to themselves than they would be in real life; for by no other means can they be made intelligible to the audience. . . . Cauchon, Lemaître [the inquisitor], and Warwick . . . were part of the Middle Ages themselves, and therefore as unconscious of its peculiarities as of the atomic formula of the air they breathed. But the play would be unintelligible if I had not endowed them with enough of this consciousness to enable them to explain their attitude to the twentieth century' (CPBS 631). He goes on to say: '. . . the things I represent these three exponents of the drama as saying are the things they actually would have said if they had known what they were really doing' (CPBS 632). In this way Shaw is able to give his audience a play of ideas and not just another romantic portrait of Saint Joan, such as those he castigates in the Preface.

Although *Saint Joan* is a play of ideas, it is predominantly of interest because it works dramatically, as all who have seen it in the theatre can testify. It has variety, humour, interesting well-drawn characters, and the action progresses clearly and inevitably towards Joan's trial. These factors, together with a mastery of language that even Shaw never surpassed, combine to make the play one that can take its place in the ranks of the outstanding dramatic productions of the 20th century.

A few references will have to suffice to indicate the play's variety. The opening scene, with its blustering humour, economically gives us the sense of desperation in which the invaded France finds herself. Some have found the ending of this scene, with the hens laying like mad, rather crude and offensive, but the point is thereby made of Joan's divine inspiration.

When the action shifts to Chinon in Scene Two Shaw is at

his best. The atmosphere of the court is skilfully evoked and the character of the Dauphin is an outstanding creation. He is one of Shaw's clever cowards, in some ways reminding one of Bentley Summerhays in *Misalliance*. What is important is to note Joan's power of putting life into this undignified figure, and her statement, 'Minding your own business is like minding your own body: it's the shortest way to make yourself sick' (CP 975), is yet another example of the doctrine that Shaw always preached —that anything worth while in this life requires risk and effort. Scene Two contains a great deal of variety within itself, moving as it does so easily from comedy to a mood of dignity and reverence. It is hard not to be moved by the Archbishop's speech of rebuke to the tittering courtiers when Joan says that it must be a wonderful thing to be an Archbishop, and yet the antics of the Dauphin do not clash with this mood.

Failures of Language

The language of the play has been justly praised; character and means of expression are carefully matched. Joan's speech is always direct, although some would wish that Shaw had not tried to indicate her rural origins by trying to write a kind of dialect for her, which results in rather unfunny 'thee's' and 'thou's' and addressing the Dauphin as 'lad' and 'Charlie'. However, I feel that it is when Shaw abandons his customary directness of style (although we should note that he often achieves this directness by rhetorical means, as in the big speech of the Inquisitor in the trial scene) that his language can be embarrassing. He attempts to be 'poetic' at the opening of Scene Three when Dunois is awaiting a west wind on the banks of the Loire, and the poeticising is out of character and therefore out of place. Another point at which I feel that the play falters in a similar way is when Joan tears up her recantation in the trial scene. Her speech about 'the wind in the trees, the larks in the sunshine, the young lambs crying through the healthy frost, and the blessed blessed church bells' (Scene Six CP 1000) seems to me to be over-written; but it is only fair to say that many find it very moving, and there have been speeches of a similar style from Joan earlier in the play.

There must be many readers of the play who find themselves irritated by Shaw's 'English' joke, as epitomised by Warwick's chaplain, de Stogumber. Throughout his life Shaw felt it necessary to point out to the English how insular they are. We can find examples of this in many of his minor plays, as well as in *Caesar and Cleopatra* and *The Man of Destiny*. Usually the joke works because the nature of the play containing it is light, but it is hard not to feel that by insisting on it in this play Shaw was making a mistake. One feels irritated by de Stogumber, although it could be argued that the discussion on nationalism requires British obstinacy to spark it off, and that he provides it. However, it is hard to accept the de Stogumber of the epilogue after what we have seen of him earlier in the play; the change is too drastic.

The Epilogue

The epilogue has always aroused a great deal of controversy as many readers feel that Shaw would have made his point more effectively if the play had ended on Warwick's 'The last of her? Hm! I wonder!' (CP 1002). They feel that although the theatrical effectiveness of the epilogue cannot be denied, it detracts from the tragic implications of the play. The mood of comedy (almost farce) generated by the appearance of the ruffianly English soldier and the gentleman who announces Joan's canonisation perhaps do prevent an easy emotional identification with Joan in the way that many playwrights would have aimed at. However, Shaw attempts a difficult feat, that of achieving seriousness in the face of comedy—and the final moments of the play are very moving. In spite of all their good wishes and congratulations none of the characters wants Joan to return to earth. Shaw ends the play on an elevated note immediately following a rather cheap laugh about the Soldier's return to Hell. Only a master playwright could manage to do that.

Joan's Character

The character of Joan as portrayed by Shaw is most appealing. He does not minimise her obstinacy and he indicates how awkward it must have been for the French commanders and dignitaries to have her playing such an important part for their cause. However, Joan's essential simplicity and honesty make us like her, and flashes of humanity, such as when she tells Dunois that she always gives sound military reasons for her actions when they are in reality inspired by her voices, add warmth to her personality. Shaw indicates why we are attracted to her when he says in the Preface that at her trial she really could not understand what she was accused of. She is an innocent who has to be sacrificed for expediency. Almost everything we have seen of her is to her credit, and the quiet dignity of her bearing both in the trial scene and in the epilogue makes us realise that here, perhaps, is the only figure in Shaw's work to whom we might consider applying the adjective 'tragic'.

5

Comedy

Earlier in this book analyses of individual plays have demonstrated the serious themes which Shaw wished to bring to public attention. We can see that he was intensely serious in his opinions, but he never allows seriousness to become solemnity; pomposity is never present in his arguments. Professor B. Ifor Evans (now Lord Evans) has overstated the case when he writes, 'Without humour, the vision of life as he saw it would have led him to the scaffold as a revolutionary' (*A Short History of English Literature*), but he is right in stressing the importance of humour in Shaw's work. For now that many of the issues about which Shaw wrote are 'dated' (for example prostitution is no longer the only way out of drudgery for a pretty working-class girl, and the sweat shops of *The Millionairess* no longer exist) it is because of their wit and humour that certain of Shaw's plays continue to hold the stage.

Inevitably some of the points to be raised in this chapter will be echoed at other points in the book, but it may be helpful to attempt to isolate here certain characteristics of Shaw's writing which help to explain his continuing reputation as a wit and humorist.

PARADOX

Time and again we cannot help being struck by Shaw's love of paradox. It is apparent in his style, and is just as marked in his characterisation. Mrs. Warren, for instance, far from being a monster or, worse still, a fallen woman with a heart of gold, is engagingly human; and the success of *Pygmalion* depends largely on the failure of Doolittle to live up to the conventional image of

93

a dustman. We realise that Shaw is trying to show in this play that it is only lack of education and opportunity that cause many of the Elizas of this world to remain flower girls: a great deal of enjoyment is gained from seeing Eliza's father, Doolittle, given the opportunity his natural ability warrants.

When he arrives at Higgins's house in Wimpole Street to attempt to blackmail the professor, his natural eloquence in explaining that he is 'one of the undeserving poor' causes Higgins to say, 'Pickering: if we were to take this man in hand for three months, he could choose between a seat in the Cabinet and a popular pulpit in Wales' (Act Two CP 730). We note already the striking equation of two positions that most of us would have thought called for rather different levels of ability, but Shaw's master stroke regarding Doolittle is saved for later in the play. After Eliza's triumphant appearance at the Embassy (incidentally, as it seems to have been an evening function, it can hardly have been 'the ambassador's garden party' that Colonel Pickering refers to in Act Two CP 723) the play enters on a calm phase. Eliza runs away to Mrs. Higgins and our attention is occupied with wondering how the Eliza/Higgins relationship will resolve itself. However, it cannot be denied that the main impetus of the play has disappeared, since everything has been leading up to the moment of Eliza's test. But Shaw gives the play an extra boost in its dying stages when he brings Doolittle on to the scene again.

In his very first play, *Widowers' Houses*, Shaw showed us a transformation scene when the downtrodden rent collector, Lickcheese, reappeared in the last act splendidly dressed as a successful, though shady, businessman. Something of the same kind happens in *Pygmalion* when Doolittle appears 'resplendently dressed as for a formal wedding' (Penguin edition 117). Higgins's joke of recommending the dustman to an American millionaire as 'the most original moralist at present in England' (Act Five CP 743) has caused him to be left £4,000 a year in the millionaire's will, on condition that he lectures for the Wannafeller Moral Reform World League as often as they ask him up to six times a year. The idea is, of course, preposterous, but Shaw makes serious use of it, as well as giving us plenty to laugh about in

Doolittle's panic-stricken reactions to his unwanted respectability. Eliza has already said in Act Two that her father prefers to work as a dustman rather than follow his proper trade as a navvy, so it would seem that he has not been exercising his talents fully even at that level. Now, however, Shaw is able to imply that only innate ability counts in a teacher or thinker, not class or upbringing. The parallel with Eliza's situation is not hard to see.

Obviously this is not all that can be said about Doolittle and his importance in the play. His way with words is most telling, as Higgins points out early on. We can see it when he tells of 'the Skilly of the workhouse and the Char Bydis of the middle class' (CP 744), and we feel comically moved by the cadences of 'Intimidated: thats what I am. Broke. Bought up. Happier men than me will call for my dust, and touch me for their tip: and I'll look on helpless, and envy them' (CP 744). The paradox of a man of his position being so fluent is matched by the paradox of his mistress and himself being so daunted by middle-class respectability that they marry in St. George's, Hanover Square, which, far from bringing them happiness, deflates them. We learn that the prospective bride 'never comes to words with anyone now, poor woman! respectability has broke all the spirit out of her' (Act Five CP 747). Perhaps the laughter this statement provokes in an audience is of a rather superior kind that we may feel should not be encouraged, but Shaw's control over language at this stage of the play, combined with this dramatic reversal of accepted codes and values, gives the play a lift and helps to round it off satisfactorily.

Higgins and Pickering

Doolittle is the most obviously 'comic' character in *Pygmalion*, but it would be a mistake to assume that all the play's laughter is associated with him. A great deal of our amusement is caused by Higgins and his outbursts. When he says of Eliza in Act Two 'She's so deliciously low—so horribly dirty—' (CP 723) we laugh almost in spite of ourselves because of his outspokenness, and it is his single-mindedness that amuses us when he instructs Mrs. Pearce to clean Eliza with Monkey Brand, burn all her clothes and wrap her up in brown paper until new ones arrive from the shop. His obsession with his profession causes him to act unconventionally at all times, sometimes very rudely. It is interesting to note how Shaw makes the best comic use of this fact. Higgins on his own would not be very funny, so Shaw has to provide characters who act as the respectable norm beside which he can be judged. Mrs. Pearce with her common sense is one of these characters, but it is necessary for the play's success for there to be another man to contrast with Higgins.

Colonel Pickering is that man and his part in the play is vital. Just as Sherlock Holmes had Doctor Watson in whom to confide his theories, thereby allowing the reader to understand the processes of the great detective's mind, so Pickering is the audience's representative in the play. Although we gather that he is an expert on Sanscrit, he merely gives the impression of being amiable and slightly stupid. His caution and good manners contrast with Higgins's volatile qualities, and help us to understand the Professor better. He admires Higgins's abilities and in the tea-party scene at Mrs. Higgins's home is quite carried away with excitement about the project of passing Eliza off as a lady, so that we have the comic spectacle of the two men shouting simultaneously about the way Eliza's education is going. Occasionally Shaw allows Pickering to make some remark that is funny in a theatrical way without being witty in itself, as in the following exchange:

MRS. HIGGINS: Colonel Pickering: dont you realise that when Eliza walked into Wimpole Street, something walked in with her?
PICKERING: Her father did. But Henry soon got rid of him.

ACT THREE CP 738

In general, however, he is the calm character who acts as a foil to Higgins and perhaps causes us to sympathise with him more than we should do otherwise; if a decent, humane man like Pickering finds Higgins amiable, perhaps we, the audience, can overlook some of his selfishness and conceit and find him likeable as well as witty.

Inevitably, in discussing a writer such as Shaw, oversimplication creeps in. Therefore we should remember that he achieves his comic effects by a variety of methods, verbal, visual, and those connected with character and situation, and at times certain of these methods of arousing laughter overlap. It is a mark of his comic genius that he has at his command so many different methods of making us laugh. He himself realised his own gifts and saw the way in which they could be best used when he wrote in the foreword to the edition of the Complete Plays: 'If I make you laugh at yourself, remember that my business as a classic writer of comedies is "to chasten morals with ridicule"; and if I sometimes make you feel like a fool, remember that I have by the same action cured your folly, just as the dentist cures your toothache by pulling out your tooth. And I never do it without giving you plenty of laughing gas' (CP vi).

Shaw may have been rather over-optimistic in assuming that folly is cured so easily, but he is certainly right about the laughing gas.

In examining certain of the effects in *Pygmalion* we have seen that much of the play's comic character depends on the appearance of the unexpected, particularly in the character of Doolittle. This love of the paradoxical is to be found in many of the other plays and is something that never failed to fascinate Shaw, even up to the appearance of his last play of real interest, *In Good King Charles's Golden Days* in 1939.

'CAESAR AND CLEOPATRA'

In *Caesar and Cleopatra*, written in 1898, Shaw presents his typically unromantic view of the relationship between those two almost legendary figures, and a large part of our amusement in watching or reading the play comes from the dry humour that Shaw attributes to Julius Caesar. His Caesar, however, is in reality a well-educated, urbane member of the English middle class of the eighteen-nineties; there is almost no attempt to make him a credible historical figure.

The Anti-English Joke

In the same way Shaw deliberately goes out of his way to create an anachronistic ancient Briton to act as secretary-companion to Caesar. The portrayal of the character of Britannus is Shaw writing at his most theatrically effective and in his most impish vein. Elsewhere I have made reference to Shaw's love of the anti-English joke. We can see it in Napoleon's long speech about the English in *The Man of Destiny*, and in de Stogumber's ridiculous attitude in *Saint Joan*. Always when he uses it Shaw can be sure of appreciation from the audience. He realised, as Shakespeare did before him, that the audience is flattered when it is most insulted. We have only to remember the gravedigger's exchange with Hamlet to see the truth of this observation. The gravedigger has just told Hamlet that he began his trade when 'our last King Hamlet overcame Fortinbras'. He continues, 'It was the very day that young Hamlet was born: he that is mad, and sent into England'.

HAMLET: Ay, marry, why was he sent into England?
CLOWN: Why, because he was mad: he shall recover his wits there; or,
    if he do not, 'tis no great matter there.
HAMLET: Why?
CLOWN: 'Twill not be seen in him there; there the men are as mad as he.
                                        HAMLET V, i, 145–50

Shaw's Britannus is an affectionate portrait, but nevertheless full of quiet irony, as we might expect from an Irishman. Britannus is completely convinced of his own rightness of judgment on every occasion, with theatrically effective, comic results. When he learns that Ptolemy and Cleopatra, who are brother and sister, are also king and consort, he is shocked into saying 'Caesar: this is not proper', thereby allowing Shaw his dry humour at the expense of the English in Caesar's reply: 'Pardon him, Theodotus: he is a barbarian, and thinks that the customs of his tribe and island are the laws of nature' (Act Two CP 265).

On another occasion Shaw has a sly dig at Britannus' political opinions, in the following exchange with Cleopatra:

CLEOPATRA: Is it true that when Caesar caught you on that island, you
    were painted all over blue?
BRITANNUS: Blue is the color worn by all Britons of good standing.
                                        ACT TWO CP 272

Constantly Britannus is convinced of the superiority of his own nation. He does not say so in a crudely direct way, but it is always evident from his manner and speech that this is his basic belief. When he has been examining the crane on the lighthouse in Act Three he tells Rufio, Caesar's general, that there are only two people to work it. Rufio is amazed: 'What! An old man and a boy work that! Twenty men, you mean.'

BRITANNUS: Two only, I assure you. They have counterweights, and a machine with boiling water in it which I do not understand: it is not of British design.   ACT THREE CP 278

What a wealth of meaning that last phrase carries.

At the end of Act Three everything is bustle and activity. Caesar, Rufio and Apollodorus swim to the ships in the east harbour to avoid being isolated on the lighthouse by the Egyptians. The urgency of the escape is given some relief by Britannus' reactions. He is scared, but remains dignified—'Caesar: I am a man and a Briton, not a fish. I must have a boat. I cannot swim' (Act Three CP 281). He remains at the lighthouse while the others go for rescue. The final words in the scene are surely Shaw being mischievous at the expense of the English public-school man whom he abhorred:

CAESAR (*swimming further off*): Take refuge up there by the beacon; and pile the fuel on the trap door, Britannus.
BRITANNUS (*calling in reply*): I will first do so, and then commend myself to my country's gods. (*A sound of cheering from the sea. Britannus gives full vent to his excitement*). The boat has reached him: Hip, hip, hip, hurrah!   ACT THREE CP 282

It is worth noting that in the serious business of Act Four Britannus is not on stage. Shaw knew how to achieve his effects, but, perhaps even more important, he also usually knew when to call a halt. In Act Four Caesar becomes aware of just how ruthless Cleopatra can be, and the scene contains two very bloody killings, even though we see only the result of the slaying of Ftatateeta, Cleopatra's nurse. It would have been inappropriate to have Britannus present in a scene of this nature, as a brooding, evil quality has to be conveyed to the audience. His next appearance is in the play's last act when a note of light-heartedness is not out of place. Caesar, about to depart for Rome, has just named Rufio as governor of the province. It is a moment of deep emotion, and Rufio 'becomes husky, and turns away to recover himself'. At this point Caesar lightens the mood by calling up Britannus:

CAESAR: Who bade you, pray, thrust yourself into the battle of the Delta, uttering the barbarous cries of your native land, and affirming yourself a match for any four of the Egyptians, to whom you applied unseemly epithets? ACT FIVE CP 295

Britannus is offered his freedom by Caesar for his bravery in the battle, but refuses it, saying 'Only as Caesar's slave have I found real freedom' (CP 295). We should note that his function in the play is rather more subtle than we might have thought at first. He is not merely a comic figure, but one worthy of respect. Although his patriotism and conservatism may cause us to smile, he is basically a worthy man whose devotion to Caesar, matched by Caesar's regard for him, causes us to reassess both characters. Obviously the prime reason for his inclusion in the play is to amuse the audience, but it is not the only reason.

The Prologue

Apart from the humour in the play linked with the characters of Caesar and Britannus, Shaw is very successful in creating amusement in the Prologue, which is spoken directly to the audience by the god Ra. The speech, which was specially written by Shaw for a revival of the play in 1913, is theatrically extremely effective from its first words—'Peace! Be silent and hearken unto me, ye quaint little islanders. Give ear, ye men with white paper on your breasts, and nothing written thereon (to signify the innocency of your minds)' (Prologue CP 250). At once Shaw has gained his audience's attention by calling them 'quaint little islanders', and the technique of insult is carried a stage further with the reference to the white shirt-fronts worn by the men in the audience.

In the Prologue Shaw gives us the historical background necessary to an understanding of the play. He realises that information given to the audience directly in a speech like this would be unacceptable unleavened by humour. So we have a Ra who wins his audience's attention by his sardonic attitude, and his references to their being in a theatre:

'Look upon my hawk's head; and know that I am Ra, who was once in Egypt a mighty god. Ye cannot kneel nor prostrate yourselves; for ye are packed in rows without freedom to move, obstructing one another's vision; neither do any of ye regard it as seemly to do ought until ye see all the rest do so too; wherefore it commonly happens that in great emergencies ye do nothing, though each telleth his fellow that something must be done. I ask you not for worship, but for silence. Let not your men speak nor your women cough; for I am come to draw you back two thousand years over the graves of sixty generations.'   PROLOGUE CP 250

The speech has some of the same quality of inviting audience participation that John Osborne achieves in his play *Luther*, in the scene where Tetzel is shown selling papal indulgences to the crowd. Shaw constantly makes his audience aware that he knows they are there, as a schoolmaster drops in a boy's name occasionally to enliven a sleepy class. Ra says:

'Hearken to me then, oh ye compulsorily educated ones. . . . Now mark me, that ye may understand what ye are presently to see. . . . And now, would ye know the end of Pompey, or will ye sleep while a god speaks?'   PROLOGUE CP 250–51

Continually contact is made between speaker and listeners; Shaw dares his audience to be inattentive:

'Are ye impatient with me? Do ye crave for a story of an unchaste woman?'   PROLOGUE CP 252

His weapons are withering irony and direct insult, which, as we have previously seen, audiences like:

'And now I leave you; for ye are a dull folk, and instruction is wasted on you. . . . Settle ye therefore in your seats and keep silent; for ye are about to hear a man speak, and a great man he was, as ye count greatness. And fear not that I shall speak to you again: the rest of the story must ye learn from them that lived it. Farewell; and do not presume to applaud me.'   PROLOGUE CP 252

The theatrical mastery shown by Shaw in the last sentence must be obvious to all. He *knows* that he has held the audience's attention throughout a long speech (it occupies more than five pages in the Penguin edition of the play). He has done so partly by the clarity of the Prologue with its measured cadences, but partly his success has been achieved by the use of humour.

Other examples of humour abound in *Caesar and Cleopatra*. It would seem only fair to record, however, one of Shaw's failures. Throughout his writing career he was addicted to the use of what he considered funny names and nicknames—we remember, for instance, B.B. in *The Doctor's Dilemma* saying that 'In moments of domestic worry, I am simple Ralph. When the sun shines in the home, I am Beedle-Deedle-Dumkins. Such is married life!' (Act Two CP 519). In *Saint Joan* the Dauphin is referred to by Joan as 'Charlie', which is bearable, but in *Caesar and Cleopatra* many people must find the recurring joke of mispronouncing Ftatateeta's name rather tiresome. However, this is a small blot on an extremely entertaining play.

'THE DOCTOR'S DILEMMA'

We have already noted several times in this chapter how Shaw often makes use of paradox for comic effect, for example presenting us with a highly articulate dustman in *Pygmalion* and with an educated, urbane slave in *Caesar and Cleopatra*. There are more examples of this technique in *The Doctor's Dilemma*, a play that has held the stage ever since its first performance in 1906, although few readers nowadays would agree with Shaw's subtitle—'A Tragedy'. There must be many who find the death of Louis Dubedat, the rascally artist of genius, singularly unmoving, and who feel that when Shaw attempts to move on to a 'poetic' level, as in Dubedat's last big speech, he is on uneasy ground. It is for the portrayal of the doctors that the play will be remembered.

The plot of *The Doctor's Dilemma* is straightforward. At the opening of the play we learn that a famous physician, Colenso Ridgeon, has been knighted for his services to medicine. He has discovered a new method of curing tuberculosis, but, as his treatment is a new one, he is only able to accept ten patients at the hospital. Among the callers on the morning that Ridgeon's knighthood is announced is Jennifer Dubedat, the wife of an artist who is dying of tuberculosis. Although Ridgeon has told her that to accept any further patients would involve withdrawing treatment from those already in hospital, he agrees to see Dubedat, partly because he is so impressed with the drawings Jennifer has brought with her to show him and partly because he is attracted by her. From this point on the play has about it the quality of a balloon debate, as we have been told that Ridgeon's ten patients were chosen for their moral worth:

'In every single one of those ten cases I have had to consider, not only whether the man could be saved, but whether he was worth saving. There were fifty cases to choose from; and forty had to be condemned to death. Some of the forty had young wives and helpless children. If the hardness of their cases could have saved them they would have been saved ten times over.'   ACT ONE CP 516

Predictably, Louis Dubedat turns out to be a scoundrel, but a charmer, and there is no doubt that his artistic talent is genuine. However, things are complicated by the fact that Blenkinsop (a poor doctor friend of Ridgeon's), a worthy man in all ways, reveals that he himself is suffering from tuberculosis. Ridgeon, appalled by Dubedat's borrowing from his guests at the dinner party, and the revelation by the hotel maid that she is Dubedat's real wife, abandoned by him after the honeymoon, is asked by Sir Patrick Cullen:

'Well, Mr Savior of Lives: which is it to be? that honest decent man Blenkinsop, or that rotten blackguard of an artist, eh?'

ACT TWO CP 524

Ridgeon reveals to Cullen that he is in love with Jennifer Dubedat and decides to take on Blenkinsop's case while turning Dubedat over to Sir Ralph Bloomfield Bonington. This is tantamount to condemning Dubedat to death, as B.B. has already shown himself in the play to be little better than a mountebank. Dubedat does die, but the final irony of the play is that Jennifer will have nothing to do with Ridgeon and marries someone else.

Regarded objectively, the plot does not hold a great deal of interest and the doctor's dilemma itself seems very contrived. The main interest of the play lies in Shaw's drawing of the characters of the doctors, and his picture of the medical profession. Doctors have always been a target of satirists, and Molière, for example, ridiculed them mercilessly in *Le Malade Imaginaire*. In *The Doctor's Dilemma* Shaw makes his points chiefly by exaggeration, particularly in the caricatured portraits of B.B. and Cutler Walpole. These two create a great deal of laughter among the audience by their insistence on their own particular panaceas —in B.B.'s case 'stimulating the phagocytes', and in Walpole's, removing the nuciform sac. It is amusing to hear the two when they are talking about their methods of treatment, and invariably, by a deflating quip at the end of their speeches, Shaw makes his own point of view obvious:

WALPOLE: Ninety-five per cent of the human race suffer from chronic blood-poisoning, and die of it. It's as simple as A.B.C. Your nuciform sac is full of decaying matter—undigested food and waste products—rank ptomaines. Now you take my advice, Ridgeon. Let me cut it out for you. Youll be another man afterwards.

SIR PATRICK: Dont you like him as he is?

WALPOLE: No I dont. I dont like any man who hasnt a healthy circulation. I tell you this: in an intelligently governed country people wouldnt be allowed to go about with nuciform sacs, making themselves centres of infection. The operation ought to be compulsory: it's ten times more important than vaccination.

SIR PATRICK: Have you had your own sac removed, may I ask?

WALPOLE (*triumphantly*): I havnt got one. Look at me! Ive no symptoms. I'm as sound as a bell.   ACT ONE CP 509–10

Walpole's obsession is obvious from the foregoing speeches. Remembering the fad (not many years ago) for removing children's tonsils when they were quite healthy, can we say that Shaw is exaggerating unduly? An extract from one of B.B.'s speeches will serve to illustrate his attitude towards medicine:

B.B.: I was put on the track by accident. I had a typhoid case and a tetanus case side by side in the hospital: a beadle and a city missionary. Think of what that meant for them, poor fellows! Can a beadle be dignified with typhoid? Can a missionary be eloquent with lockjaw? No. NO. Well, I got some typhoid anti-toxin from Ridgeon and a tube of Muldooley's anti-tetanus serum. But the missionary jerked all my things off the table in one of his paroxysms; and in replacing them I put Ridgeon's tube where Muldooley's ought to have been. The consequence was that I inoculated the typhoid case for tetanus and the tetanus case for typhoid. (*The doctors look greatly concerned. B.B., undamped, smiles triumphantly*). Well, they recovered. THEY RECOVERED. Except for a touch of St. Vitus's dance the missionary's as well today as ever; and the beadle's ten times the man he was. ACT ONE CP 513–14

The humour in this speech is generated by B.B.'s use of rhetoric. His own inherent sense of drama gives the speech its build-up, and Shaw releases tension at the end (after the stage direction) by B.B.'s casual reference to the missionary's 'touch of St. Vitus's dance'. It is obvious, however, that Shaw is deeply concerned by the paradox of the existence of the clever fool in the medical world. His presentation of Walpole and B.B. shows this, but to counterbalance them he has given us Sir Patrick Cullen and Ridgeon. These two are honest men, and Sir Patrick is particularly important in the play for his ability to put things in historical perspective. He knows that medicine works in cycles, that methods of treatment come into fashion and then go out again. His dry wit and honesty are a great contribution to the play.

B.B. and Walpole are the two most eminent doctors who call to congratulate Ridgeon in the first act. However, it would be a mistake to think that Shaw is only satirising the medical profession at its Harley Street level. Dr. Schutzmacher is shown to have prospered in general practice by advertising 'Cure Guaranteed' and prescribing Parrish's Chemical Food for his patients. Blenkinsop, a kindly, straightforward man with a poor little practice, is shown to be a rather incompetent doctor. He confesses to not having opened a book since he qualified thirty years before, and he prescribes for his poor patients 'a pound of ripe greengages every day half an hour before lunch' (Act One CP 513). Shaw is obviously sympathetic towards Blenkinsop, but the implications are obvious: that medicine should be taken out of the realms of private practice, so that the Blenkinsops of the world need no longer bother whether the treatment they prescribe for their shopmen and clerks is expensive or not, and so that charlatans like B.B. and Walpole will be driven to making an honest living.

Although the play has these serious undertones it is perhaps for its many medical jokes that it will continue to be performed. We remember for instance:

B.B. (*sadly*): Walpole has no intellect. A mere surgeon. Wonderful operator; but, after all, what is operating? Only manual labor.

ACT ONE CP 514

and a little later:

B.B.: Goodbye, Ridgeon. Dont fret about your health: you know what to do: if your liver is sluggish, a little mercury never does any harm. If you feel restless, try bromide. If that doesnt answer a stimulant, you know: a little phosphorus and strychnine. If you cant sleep, trional, trional, trion—

SIR PATRICK (*dryly*): But no drugs, Colly, remember that.

B.B. (*firmly*): Certainly not. Quite right, Sir Patrick. As temporary expedients, of course; but as treatment, no, NO. Keep away from the chemist's shop, my dear Ridgeon, whatever you do.

ACT ONE CP 514

Other methods of raising a laugh in the play are numerous. We recall the low comedy turn of Emmy, Ridgeon's housekeeper, in the first act, and the rebuff suffered by the unfortunate Redpenny when he enters to interrupt Ridgeon's conversation with Jennifer when that is precisely what he has been told to do. It would not do, however, to overlook the contribution that Dubedat makes to the amusement caused by the play. He is not merely the instrument for revealing further the obsessions of the doctors about which we have learned earlier. He is well able to cause laughter himself.

Readers and audiences have always liked a rogue, as we know from the reception given to such figures as Parolles, in *All's Well That Ends Well*, Pickwick's friend, Mr. Jingle, and Evelyn Waugh's Basil Seal. In spite of the fact that these characters would be unpleasant to deal with in real life, they captivate us when we meet them on the stage or on the printed page. It is their effrontery and belief in their own qualities that make them tolerable, and perhaps we sublimate our own less creditable desires in observing their actions. We feel that the Basil Seals of the world are not mean characters—their attempts at swindling are usually on the grand scale, and they do not act in a hypocritical fashion. Dubedat belongs to this class, talking money out of B.B. and Walpole at the dinner party by appealing to their vanity; we feel more critical of him, however, when he 'borrows' half a crown from Blenkinsop on the pretext of wanting 'to tip the chambermaid of the room his wife left her wraps in, and for the cloakroom' (Act Two CP 521).

In the scene in Dubedat's studio (Act Three) we see him as he really is—quite amoral. He obviously feels no gratitude towards the doctors for taking on his case, telling Jennifer '. . . I daresay they think it will be a feather in their cap to cure a rising artist' (CP 526). However, in the course of the scene we have to award Louis our grudging admiration for being so completely true to himself. There is no attempt to conceal his awfulness. For example he suggests to Ridgeon that he might persuade some of his patients to buy some drawings or give him some portrait commissions, as 'You must know such lots of things about them —private things that they wouldnt like to have known. They wouldnt dare to refuse you' (CP 527). He goes on to give Walpole a pawn-ticket when called on to restore the cigarette case 'borrowed' at the *Star and Garter*. This action is very amusing on stage, as anyone who has seen the play will be able to confirm, but there are better things to come, for example his borrowing of half a crown from Walpole to settle his debt to Dr. Blenkinsop.

As the scene progresses Dubedat remorselessly gains the upper hand, even egging on B.B. when the latter expresses a desire to take him by the scruff of the neck and give him a sound thrashing, saying, 'I wish you would. Youd pay me something handsome to keep it out of court afterwards' (CP 530). This constant putting down of the doctors by the villain of the play keeps the audience amused, although there is little that is specifically witty about the speeches themselves. It is the way in which Dubedat maintains his effrontery without even seeming to recognise that he is being outrageous that causes our laughter:

LOUIS (*changing color*): Do you mean, operate on me? Ugh! No, thank you.
WALPOLE: Never fear: you wont feel anything. Youll be under an anaesthetic, of course. And it will be extraordinarily interesting.
LOUIS: Oh, well, if it would interest you, and if it wont hurt, thats another matter. How much will you give me to let you do it?

ACT THREE CP 531

B.B. takes on Dubedat's case when he has been rejected by Ridgeon and Walpole. It is good to see the seemingly woolly-minded Sir Ralph defeat Dubedat over the matter of the sketch of Sir Patrick Cullen. Dubedat thinks he has sold the portrait to B.B. for twelve guineas, only to hear the reply: 'I neednt settle with you now, Mr Dubedat: my fees will come to more than that' (Act Three CP 532).

The act ends more seriously with the conversation between Ridgeon and Jennifer, who so obviously loves her husband while knowing little or nothing of his real nature. Even in this conversation there is humour of a sort, with the irony of Ridgeon's being unable to speak ill of Dubedat to Jennifer when she challenges him to do so. In the fourth act Shaw is chiefly preoccupied with writing Dubedat's death scene, but the bickering of B.B. and Walpole is still in evidence. We now see the serious consequences behind the amusingly presented obsessions. However, the scene contains one or two episodes or remarks in a lighter vein. B.B.'s absurd misquotations of Shakespeare give some comic relief, as does Walpole's follow-up to Sir Paddy's 'No matter: it's not for us to judge. He's in another world now.'

WALPOLE: Borrowing his first five-pound note there, probably.

ACT FOUR CP 540

The play ends on an ironic note. Ridgeon in turning Dubedat's case over to B.B., did so knowing that Louis was almost certain to die as a result. Nevertheless, his stratagem to marry Jennifer fails, and the last laugh in the play is a bitter one when Jennifer tells Ridgeon that she has already married again, causing him to say: 'Then I have committed a purely disinterested murder!' (Act Five CP 546). Once again Shaw has produced the unexpected to startle us.

The play has survived now for more than sixty years, and shows no sign of becoming out-dated, although it is obviously in some ways a period piece. It should continue to hold the stage because of its portrayals of the wrangling medical men, who demonstrate the truth of Sir Patrick Cullen's statement in the first act, that 'All professions are conspiracies against the laity' (CP 515). Shaw's point is that such a conspiracy in the medical profession is one that we can ill afford; his main weapon in driving home this point is humour.

'HEARTBREAK HOUSE'

Although Shaw began *Heartbreak House* before the First World War, it was not performed until 1919. He explains in the Preface why he left it unproduced. During the war the theatre audiences were composed of soldiers in search of very light entertainment, and, in any case, Shaw felt that 'comedy, though sorely tempted, had to be loyally silent' (CPBS 399). He recognised the absurdities of war, yet saw that 'When men are heroically dying for their country, it is not the time to shew their lovers and wives and fathers and mothers how they are being sacrificed to the blunders of boobies . . .' (CPBS 399). For this reason it seemed impolitic to put on a play which ends with a Zeppelin raid, and which shows metaphorically the moral worthlessness of the cultivated English middle class of the day. Captain Shotover rather cryptically points the way to salvation in one of the last exchanges of the play:

HECTOR: And this ship that we are all in? This soul's prison we call England?

CAPTAIN SHOTOVER: The captain is in his bunk, drinking bottled ditchwater; and the crew is gambling in the forecastle. She will strike and sink and split. Do you think the laws of God will be suspended in favor of England because you were born in it?

HECTOR: Well, I dont mean to be drowned like a rat in a trap. I still have the will to live. What am I to do?

CAPTAIN SHOTOVER: Do? Nothing simpler. Learn your business as an Englishman.

HECTOR: And what may my business as an Englishman be, pray?

CAPTAIN SHOTOVER: Navigation. Learn it and live; or leave it and be damned. ACT THREE CP 801

The captain's statement of the situation, taken together with the fact that the bomb dropped by the Zeppelin kills the burglar and Boss Mangan, the two outstanding parasites in the play, points forward to a time when England will be governed according to sound economic and social principles and reminds the reader of similar speeches in the plays of the Russian dramatist, Chekhov (1860–1904). Trofimov, the eternal student in *The Cherry Orchard*, looks forward to a time when social equality will be found in Russia, and Toozenbach in *Three Sisters* (written in 1900) talks in such a way as to make us feel that Chekhov definitely foresaw the Russian Revolution:

'The time's come: there's a terrific thundercloud advancing upon us, a mighty storm is coming to freshen us up! Yes, it's coming all right, it's quite near already, and it's going to blow away all this idleness and indifference, and prejudice against work, this rot of boredom that our society is suffering from. I'm going to work, and in twenty-five or thirty years' time every man and woman will be working. Every one of us!' THREE SISTERS, Act One

It is not only in its political and social implications that *Heartbreak House* reminds one of Chekhov's plays. Shaw deliberately set out to write 'A Fantasia in the Russian Manner on English Themes'. He writes in his Preface of the way in which Chekhov deals with charming people who are unfitted for dealing with the practical world. He describes how he felt that 'these intensely Russian plays fitted all the country houses in Europe in which the pleasures of music, art, literature, and the theatre had supplanted hunting, shooting, fishing, flirting, eating and drinking. The same nice people, the same utter futility' (CPBS 378). The chief crime of the inhabitants of these country houses was moral lethargy, as they hated politics and did not wish to improve the lot of the common people. In *Heartbreak House* Shaw endeavours to create a recognisably Chekhovian world, and to point out the dangers inherent in the situation he describes. The result is one of his finest comedies.

The play is set in the house of Shotover, an eightyeight-year-old retired sea-captain. The house has been built to resemble a ship, and it is used by Shaw as a symbol for the drifting, purposeless state of England prior to the First World War. Most of the characters who inhabit Shotover's house or who come to it as visitors during the action of the play are bored by having nothing useful to do. Several of them have their hearts broken, to a greater or a lesser degree, but, as a result of having what Shaw sees as their harmful illusions smashed, they are able to find some useful purpose in life. Only those who set their minds to something (like the Captain and Ellie Dunn) escape boredom, and, in Shaw's opinion, achieve self-knowledge and, with it, salvation. (It is worth noting that the something on which the characters of whom Shaw approves set their minds has to be visionary or useful to mankind. The Captain has his inventions; Hector has his desire to be used. Boss Mangan has, in his way, worked hard, but he is a parasite and is finally killed. Mazzini Dunn, Ellie's father, is another who has worked hard, yet he is portrayed as rather ineffectual and lacking in awareness, as is shown by his readiness to allow his daughter to marry Mangan. Therefore Mazzini is not finally quite accepted by Shaw as one of the play's life-enhancing figures. He is not relegated to the Mangan/Burglar class, but is kept outside the charmed circle of the Captain, Ellie, Hector and Hesione.)

Heartbreak House is really a series of conversation pieces. Often only two characters are on stage exchanging views. The pace of the play is slow, but never boring, and here again Shaw seems to have learned from Chekhov. These conversation pieces are cleverly interspersed with startling incidents, such as the discovery of the burglar, a trick that Shaw had used before (in *Misalliance*, where he has an intruder hiding in the portable Turkish bath), and humour is seldom absent. Shaw uses it to present an affectionate yet critical look at the English middle class in the last stable period it has experienced. Except in the pages of P. G. Wodehouse, the English country house weekend all but disappeared after the First World War. Shaw, like Chekhov, was critical of the inhabitants of his country house, but recognised their charm.

The humour of the play stems largely from the variety of its characters and the exaggerated positions they take up. All of the characters, with the exception of Randall Utterword and Ellie, are colourful in a way that is almost grotesque. Captain Shotover punctuates the action of the play by the way in which he tosses in outrageous statements, and then runs away before any reply can be made to them. Ellie notices this gambit:

ELLIE: You shall not run away before you answer. I have found out that trick of yours.   ACT TWO CP 789

Shotover tells her that he runs off to obtain a regular glass of rum.

The Captain has a romantic past in which he is supposed to have sold his soul to the devil in Zanzibar, and a great deal of laughter is caused by his insistence that Ellie's father, the highly respectable Mazzini Dunn, is his one-time boatswain who had previously been a pirate. The arrival late in the play of the burglar who turns out to be this same boatswain is a coincidence that we have to accept for the sake of the plot. It is interesting that both of the characters concerning whom there is a confusion of identity, Mazzini and Hector (who has claimed to be Marcus Darnley) are linked with Ellie, who, in her bewilderment at the outcome of events, can be seen as the audience's representative in the play.

The Captain's epigrammatic statements add greatly to the humour of the play, but in addition the character is used to

remind the audience of at least two other patriarchal figures—
Noah and King Lear. His exchange with Ellie in Act One, in
which he says of the boatswain Dunn:

> 'He must be greatly changed. Has he attained the seventh degree of
> concentration? ... But how could he, with a daughter? I, madam,
> have two daughters.'   CP 759

reminds the reader forcibly of Shakespeare's daughter-afflicted
King Lear. The result is to add stature to Shotover so that we
listen attentively to his apocalyptic statements later in the play,
even though we may laugh at him at other times.

The two daughters of Shotover cause amusement in very
differing ways. Hesione is the unshockable society hostess who
rightly says to Mazzini in Act Two:

> 'Now if *I* said that, it would sound witty.'   CP 779

She controls everyone, including her philandering husband
Hector, and shows her cleverness both in her quick retorts and
in the way she manipulates Boss Mangan so that he will not marry
Ellie Dunn.

Her sister Ariadne, Lady Utterword, arrives without warning
at the house after an absence of many years. The Captain says of
her:

> 'I have a second daughter who is, thank God, in a remote part of the
> Empire with her numskull of a husband. As a child she thought the
> figure-head of my ship, the Dauntless, the most beautiful thing on
> earth. He resembled it. He had the same expression: wooden yet
> enterprising. She married him. . . .'   ACT ONE CP 759

One of the play's most effective moments is when Ariadne,
having already been ignored by Captain Shotover, who refuses
to recognise her as his daughter, goes unrecognised once more,
this time by her sister:

MRS. HUSHABYE: Oh! youve brought someone with you. Introduce
  me.
LADY UTTERWORD: Hesione: is it possible that you dont know me?
MRS. HUSHABYE (*conventionally*): Of course I remember your face quite
  well. Where have we met?   ACT ONE CP 762

Ariadne is extremely conventional and much of the play's humour stems from her reactions to what she sees as the 'disorder in ideas, in talk, in feeling' in Shotover's house:

LADY UTTERWORD (*rising suddenly and explosively*): Hesione: are you going to kiss me or are you not?
MRS. HUSHABYE: What do you want to be kissed for?
LADY UTTERWORD: I *dont* want to be kissed; but I do want you to behave properly and decently. We are sisters. We have been separated for twenty-three years. You *ought* to kiss me.   ACT ONE CP 762

Throughout the play Ariadne is the prototype reactionary, referring with pride to her colonial governor husband when the burglar is caught:

'If you were a native, and Hastings could order you a good beating and send you away, I shouldnt mind; but here in England there is no real protection for any respectable person.'   ACT TWO CP 785

She believes that the chief thing wrong with Shotover's house is that there are no proper stables—'There are only two classes in good society in England: the equestrian classes and the neurotic classes. It isnt mere convention: everybody can see that the people who hunt are the right people and the people who dont are the wrong ones' (Act Three CP 795).

The audience is able to laugh at these illiberal sentiments while realising just how characteristic of a certain species of aristocrat they were and are. When considering Ariadne's contribution to the play we should note Shaw's use of the 'crying man joke' in connection with her admirer, Randall. He is Ariadne's brother-in-law and claims to love her 'In a higher sense—in a Platonic sense'. Hector's answer is to the point:

HECTOR: Psha! Platonic sense! She makes you her servant; and when pay-day comes round, she bilks you: that is what you mean.
                                        ACT TWO CP 794

Randall is the least colourful character in the play and seems to be there merely to make the numbers up, and to provide the haunting flute accompaniment in the last act. However, Shaw causes him to cry like a child towards the end of the second act, and Ariadne explains that when Randall 'gets nerves and is naughty, I just rag him til he cries' (Act Two CP 793). When we remember how Bentley Summerhays in *Misalliance* also breaks down and blubs for comic effect we can see how different Shaw's sense of humour could be on occasion from our own.

Hector as Shaw's Spokesman

Hector Hushabye represents, in Shaw's view, the best side of middle-class values. Kept almost as a pet by his wife, and, not to put too fine a point on it, a lying philanderer, he nevertheless searches for some purpose in life. In his conversation with Shotover in Act One he shows that he despises 'Mangan's bristles' and 'Randall's lovelocks' equally. He is unhappy in his present situation, telling Hesione 'I might as well be your lapdog' (Act One CP 774), and the handsome Arab costume he wears instead of conventional evening dress in Act Two is obviously indicative of a romantic longing for something positive to do. It is he who is first to dash out to confront the burglar, and when the Zeppelin comes at the end of the play he switches on all the lights in the house to attract the attention of the Germans. Even though the phrasing and balance of some of his speeches, taken together with his rakish attitude, causes us amusement, Hector is chiefly important as Shaw's spokesman in the play. He takes the rumbling of the airship to be 'Heaven's threatening growl of disgust at us useless futile creatures', and continues:

'I tell you, one of two things must happen. Either out of that darkness some new creation will come to supplant us as we have supplanted the animals, or the heavens will fall in thunder and destroy us.'   ACT THREE CP 794

Shaw is here pointing to the end of the long Edwardian afternoon, and Hector reinforces the point when he says:

'We have been too long here. We do not live in this house: we haunt it.'   ACT THREE CP 799

Despite Hector's self-disgust and the sense of deflation he feels when the house is left intact after the bombing, it is evident that Shaw thinks something can be made of the Hectors of the world.

If they would show awareness of the dangers of sheltering behind middle-class wealth and idleness, and display some of the qualities of daring associated with the Hector of the Trojan War, they could emerge as valuable leaders.

Three characters in *Heartbreak House* lie outside the social sphere of the others: Mangan, Nurse Guinness and the burglar. Nurse Guinness occupies the privileged position of trusted, slightly eccentric old servant that we find in Chekhov's *Uncle Vanya* and *Three Sisters*, and her reactions to Lady Utterword and the burglar provide humour. Lady Utterword is on her dignity when she arrives at the house and is appalled to be addressed familiarly by her old nurse:

LADY UTTERWORD: Nurse: will you please remember that I am Lady Utterword, and not Miss Addy, nor lovey, nor darling, nor doty? Do you hear?

NURSE: Yes, ducky: all right. I'll tell them all they must call you my lady.   ACT ONE CP 761

She obviously does not feel *herself* bound by the necessity to call Ariadne 'my lady'.

The speeches of Nurse Guinness are not intended to be witty, but by their forthrightness they generate amusement. The burglar turns out to be the boatswain Billy Dunn and Nurse Guinness's husband. Her comment when Dunn is led below stairs to stay with the servants is well placed to get a laugh before the play turns again towards discussion:

GUINNESS: Why didnt you shoot him, sir? If I'd known who he was, I'd have shot him myself.   ACT TWO CP 787

After this outburst it is no surprise that she greets the death of her husband in the gravel pit with 'hideous triumph' (Act Three CP 802).

The entry of the burglar in the second act can be seen as an attempt to enliven the action of what is basically a discussion play. Shaw is fond of this kind of diversion; in *Misalliance*, apart from the intruder in the Turkish bath, he has two aviators enter the action after crashing their plane into Tarleton's greenhouse.

However, the burglar in *Heartbreak House* is closely integrated into the plot and symbolism of the play. He is the husband of the Nurse and that same Billy Dunn the Captain has been taking Mazzini for throughout the play. This is, of course, a preposterous coincidence, and Shaw makes the burglar an even more incredible character by causing him to disclose that he is a deliberately incompetent house-breaker. His scheme is to 'break into the house; put a few spoons or diamonds in my pocket; make a noise; get caught; and take up a collection' (Act Two CP 787).

Brigid Brophy, in 1967, in her play *The Burglar*, appears to acknowledge the dramatic effectiveness of Shaw's intruders by taking over the device. Her play has other close parallels with Shaw. It is chiefly dependent for its interest on discussion, rather than action; its basic ingredient is paradox, containing as it does a morally-minded burglar who is extremely shocked by the sexual behaviour of those he wishes to burgle, and a husband and wife who act in a 'civilised' manner towards each other's lovers, instead of being angry; the final reminder of Shaw is the fact that Miss Brophy includes in the printed edition a fortyseven-page preface in which she sketches in the stage history of the play and elaborates on its central point.

Mangan, The Second Burglar

Boss Mangan has been mentioned as the third character who lies outside the social sphere of most of those in the play. He is the fiftyfive-year-old self-made business man who is going to try to marry Ellie, and although we find the prospect distasteful we warm towards him at certain points in the play. He is linked with the burglar as a parasite at the end when they are killed by the bomb which explodes in the gravel pit, yet it is hard not to feel a certain respect for him even when he causes us to laugh most, and at times he becomes almost human. He manages to shame Hesione by telling her in Act Two that no decent woman would have led him on while thinking him beneath contempt, but we chiefly remember Mangan for situations in which humour, not pathos, is the outcome.

When the burglar is captured and refuses the offer of escape before the police come, Mangan gets a laugh by stating what is in the minds of the audience:

THE BURGLAR (*inexorably*): No. I must work my sin off my conscience. This has come as a sort of call to me. Let me spend the rest of my life repenting in a cell. I shall have my reward above.
MANGAN (*exasperated*): The very burglars cant behave naturally in this house.   ACT TWO CP 785

The remark is skilfully placed by Shaw to trigger off laughter, particularly as it has to be delivered in an explosive fashion, but it is also indicative of Mangan's basically conventional nature. He is divided from the rest of the house-party not only by his social class but by his inability to be flexible in his reactions. It is significant that he over-reacts as a result of his realisation of his exclusion. In the last act Ellie has a speech in which she sadly comments on her crumbling illusions, and says that things in Heartbreak House have not proved to be what they seemed. She mentions Lady Utterword's false hair and Shotover's addiction to rum, and they accept it without argument. Mangan (perhaps because he is the character in the play who most readily comes to mind as being unable to face the truth squarely) says 'wildly' 'Look here: I'm going to take off all my clothes', and he begins tearing off his coat. He continues: 'Let's all strip stark naked. We may as well do the thing thoroughly when we're about it. Weve stripped ourselves morally naked: well, let us strip ourselves physically naked as well, and see how we like it' (Act Three CP 797). It is a very funny sequence, but underlines Shaw's point that Mangan is unable to face reality. Nevertheless, he has not been presented as a wicked character, and those who have seen the part well played will testify to the fact that not everybody is glad at the end of the play when he is killed in order to fit Shaw's symbolic design.

Heartbreak House is one of Shaw's most successful plays and one that will surely continue to be revived. It has variety of characters, generosity, power of rhetoric, and a pervading humour that is nearly always at the service of Shaw's main themes. In this play he seems to have been able to resist the temptation to drop in irrelevant jokes merely because they are effective at the moment, and, perhaps for this reason, many who do not usually warm to Shaw's work find *Heartbreak House* impressive.

In this chapter I have attempted to show, by an examination of certain comic techniques at work in four of Shaw's major plays, *Pygmalion*, *Caesar and Cleopatra*, *The Doctor's Dilemma*, and *Heartbreak House*, how he aimed to teach through laughter. When he is writing at his best, his comedy is disciplined and directed towards the overall aim of the play in hand. Usually his technique is to take a situation and stand it on its head (his dustman has an original mind; his Caesar wins victories through guile rather than physical bravery; some of his doctors are pompous quacks) and after that initial shock to his audience he proceeds to delight us by his sheer powers of language.

It must be emphasised that Shaw used comedy as his medium throughout his career as a dramatist, and that these four plays have been discussed as examples only. Even in his two earliest plays, *Widowers' Houses* and *Mrs. Warren's Profession*, when he was, as Edmund Wilson has pointed out in *The Triple Thinkers*, writing his only straight socialist drama, he used humour as a method of sweetening the pill of his message, as we can see if we think of the presentation of the characters of Cokane, Lickcheese and Frank Gardner. In later plays and playlets he was to use exaggeration and burlesque for comic effect. In *O'Flaherty, V.C.* and *Augustus Does His Bit*, both minor plays, political figures and army types are parodied, and many readers will remember the satirical portrayal of the trade union leader, Boanerges, in *The Apple Cart*.

PURE FUN

These examples are mostly used by Shaw to make a serious point—in *O'Flaherty, V.C.* to show the inability of the officer class to understand the outlook of the ordinary soldier, and in *The Apple Cart* to point out the dangers of letting a demagogue have political power. In some of the plays, however, comedy is used for pure fun. It would be easy to find instances in Shaw's plays at almost any point in his career. Two examples will suffice, one from *The Simpleton of the Unexpected Isles*, written in 1934, and the other from *In Good King Charles's Golden Days*, which was Shaw's last really acceptable full-length play, and was written in 1939.

In *The Simpleton of the Unexpected Isles*, the angel who has been sent to announce the Day of Judgment takes off with 'a noise like a vacuum cleaner' (Act Two CP 1242), and is too sophisticated to accept the piety of those he has visited:

VASHTI: Excelsior.

ALL FOUR (*rising and singing vociferously*): Eck-cel-see-orr! Eck-cel-see-or!
THE ANGEL (*putting his fingers in his ears*): Please, no. In heaven we are
    tired of singing. It is not done now.   ACT TWO CP 1242

In Good King Charles's Golden Days is described by Shaw as 'A True History That Never Happened'. Among the characters who meet King Charles II is Isaac Newton, the great mathematician. His housekeeper asks him to check the washing bill. Newton is unable to reply immediately, and reaches the answer in the following way:

NEWTON: You add the logarithms of the numbers; and the antilogarithm
    of the sum of the two is the answer. Let me see: three times seven?
    The logarithm of three must be decimal four seven seven or
    thereabouts. . . .   ACT ONE CP 1335

He continues, but is beaten to the answer by an uneducated fish hawker!

Various aspects of Shaw's attitude to comedy have been touched on in this chapter. It is worth noting, however, that wit and humour are his chief tools in such plays as *Man and Superman* and *Androcles and the Lion*, which are examined elsewhere. It is impossible to deal with the content of these plays without some discussion of the way Shaw achieves the effects he intends. Accordingly, this chapter on comedy is not meant to be exhaustive.

6

Characterisation

An American critic, Walter Starkie, in his book, *Luigi Pirandello, 1867–1936*, commenting on Shaw's ability to create credible characters, says that Shaw's psychology is superior to that of Ibsen, since he portrays the type, whereas Ibsen merely portrays the individual. Leaving aside discussion of the word 'merely' in that judgment, we are left with an unusual viewpoint, as readers and playgoers who are critical of Shaw often *complain* of what they see as his refusal or inability to draw individual characters, saying that he only creates mouthpieces for his debate-dramas, or is content to produce puppets for the sake of his plot. The accusations merit consideration.

Although we have seen elsewhere in this book that Shaw could create rounded, life-like characters such as Higgins, Eliza and Major Barbara, when he wished to do so, there is some truth in the charge that he sometimes created cardboard figures as mouthpieces for his ideas. This is particularly the case in some of the later plays where Shaw's interest in the ideas he was expounding got out of hand and led him to use the theatre as a platform from which to sermonise. The rather tedious debates contained in plays such as *On the Rocks* and *The Simpleton of the Unexpected Isles* read better than they act, and might make good radio drama, but they contain insufficient material that is theatrically effective. Those who have seen the 'Don Juan in Hell' section from *Man and Superman* acted divorced from the surrounding framework of the play will testify, however, that its interest is not lessened by the static form of the debate-drama. We are forced to the conclusion that it is the liveliness of the ideas and the variety of their presentation that matters and, unfortunately,

Shaw's powers were beginning to fail in the 1930s, even though certain plays, such as *Village Wooing* and *In Good King Charles's Golden Days*, which were written during that decade, are still of interest.

When we consider Shaw's drama as a whole we are reminded forcibly that he was above all a writer of plays of social protest. He was always aware of the theatre as an instrument for advocating the improvement of social conditions, and in this book, particularly in the chapters on Shaw's earliest plays and on his use of comedy, attention has been drawn to his insistence on the power of his plays to help to reform evil conditions. In many of his plays Shaw creates characters whose prime reason for existence is to put forward his own ideas or to embody rigidly defined attitudes, but we nevertheless believe in them while they are on stage. In *Mrs. Warren's Profession*, for example, Mrs. Warren is a skilfully drawn *type* whose main function is to draw attention to the evils of prostitution; in *The Doctor's Dilemma* the various doctors present the ridiculous medical theories current at the time the play was written; in *Major Barbara* Undershaft exists primarily to expound Shaw's views on the necessity for a man to have bread before religion can mean anything to him. The liveliness with which these characters are presented, even though they may sometimes be acting as mouthpieces for Shaw's own ideas, or acting as spokesmen for viewpoints that are then to be smashed down by another character, causes the audience to accept them as credible for the time that they are on stage, and must lead a thoughtful reader to examine what he may reasonably expect from a dramatist's characterisation.

In Victorian times and in the early years of this century it was customary for critics of Shakespeare, such as A. C. Bradley, to discuss the characters in his plays as though they were real people. In fact, the attitude was taken to such extremes by certain writers that Professor L. C. Knights was to write ironically about it in an article entitled 'How Many Children Had Lady Macbeth?' (1933). The great Russian actor and director, Stanislavsky (1863–1938), encouraged the actors in his productions to imagine what happened to characters they were playing when they were off the stage, and even in situations which had nothing to do with the particular play in which they were appearing. These are surely wrong approaches to stage characterisation, for, while it is generally true to say that characters in plays must bear some resemblance to living human beings, it is equally true to say that the writing of plays is an art and that many playwrights, including Shakespeare, try to do much more than merely present an imitation of ordinary life on stage.

Even a writer like Harold Pinter, the author of *The Birthday Party* and *The Caretaker*, who has recorded certain speech rhythms (usually from society's underprivileged classes) so accurately that people sometimes speak of overhearing a 'Pinter-esque' conversation on a bus, does not merely record without selection. Like Noël Coward, who succeeded in capturing the essence of the bright, clipped chatter of the upper classes of the 1920s, he has given us the essence of the people about whom he writes. It would be very boring (not to say disjointed) to be presented—in a play—with speech set down with the accuracy of a tape-recorder. It is the business of the artist to impose order on his material, and, in the cases of Pinter and Shakespeare, to give us a credible but not absolutely naturalistic picture of, for example, the Caretaker or Macbeth.

Fashions change, in literary criticism as in everything else, and it is dangerous to assume that the most modern critical attitudes are necessarily the best. Nevertheless, it is worth noting that in recent years many critics of Shakespeare have moved away from the attitude which regarded his characters as real people, and they have tended to consider his plays more from the point of view of themes and images. For example, *Measure for Measure* has been seen as a play in which the topics of authority, justice and mercy are of prime importance, and *The Merchant of Venice* as a play which is completely steeped in the language of commerce. Critics claim that all events and characters within the plays must have been manipulated by Shakespeare to fit in with the main current of ideas that interested him while he was writing. It would thus be highly dangerous to assume that Shakespeare's characters have a life independent of the plays in which they appear. The same can usually be said of the characters created by any serious playwright, and it is certainly true in the case of Shaw.

THE IMPORTANCE OF THEME

Although it would diminish Shaw's plays to say that they were solely 'about' a certain topic, it would be possible to say, for example, that *Widowers' Houses* deals chiefly with the question of slum landlords, that *Major Barbara* is mainly concerned with poverty and religion, that *The Apple Cart* is a consideration of monarchy and democracy. Obviously therefore, if Shaw was writing to promote a particular point of view in his plays, his creation of character would be subservient to his themes. Occasionally a character appears to have such vitality that he breaks away from the bounds of the play and seems to achieve a life of his own. Reference to two examples will show that this is not in fact the case, but that the impression has been cunningly fostered by the author to maintain the interest of the audience at a point where the play might otherwise flag. In short, structure is more important than characterisation.

In *You Never Can Tell*, the fourth of Shaw's Pleasant Plays, written in 1897, the most interesting character is William, the waiter at the Marine Hotel. Just as Enry Straker, in *Man and Superman*, is shown to be better educated for life in the 20th century than his master and his friends, so in this play also Shaw reverses the traditionally accepted roles of servant and employers. In spite of occupying a relatively humble position in society, William is wiser than most of the guests he has to serve at the hotel, and his opinion is asked on trifling or important matters alike. Early in Act Two, in the course of the luncheon party, there occurs a conversation that is important for two reasons. Firstly it reinforces a favourite idea of Shaw's, one on which the whole plot of *Pygmalion*, for example, is built—that social opportunity enables a person to fulfil his or her potential, no matter what his or her origins are. Secondly, the character of William's barrister son is 'planted' in the minds of the audience, so that they will not be too surprised when he appears as the 'deux ex machina' in the last act of the play.

DOLLY: Is your son a waiter too, William?

WAITER (*serving* GLORIA *with fowl*): Oh no, miss: he's too impetuous. He's at the Bar.

M'COMAS (*patronizingly*): A potman, eh?

WAITER (*with a touch of melancholy, as if recalling a disappointment softened by time*): No, sir: the other bar. *Your* profession, sir. A Q.C., sir.

M'COMAS (*embarrassed*): I'm sure I beg your pardon.

WAITER: Not at all, sir. Very natural mistake, I'm sure, sir. Ive often wished he *was* a potman, sir. Would have been off my hands ever so much sooner, sir. . . .   ACT TWO CP 191

This son dominates the last act of the play, which has an air of carnival about it. It is hardly necessary to recount the plot here. All that need be remembered is that the play concerns the fortunes of Mrs. Clandon, her three children, and Fergus Crampton, who is Mrs. Clandon's estranged husband. After eighteen years of separation he wants a reconciliation which she is reluctant to allow. If she refuses he will demand the custody of the two younger children, who are not of age. Mrs. Clandon's solicitor, Finch M'Comas, suggests that Mrs. Clandon and her husband obtain counsel's opinion on the matter. He is luckily able to arrange for his suggestion to be carried out almost immediately. An eminent barrister is staying at the seaside resort in which the play takes place, and he has offered to help with his advice. A meeting is arranged for nine o'clock. Act Three ends on a note of bustle. William, the waiter, informs the company that there is to be a fancy dress ball in the hotel that evening, and the young people, to their mother's consternation, are much more interested in this news than in meeting a lawyer at a gathering that may well decide their future.

BOHUN

The fancy dress ball of Act Four puts the audience in the mood to expect anything to happen. The behaviour of the young Clandons is partly responsible for this, especially with Phil, dressed as a harlequin, at one point waving his bat and seeming to cast a spell on the characters around him. However, it is mainly through the way in which the rather cardboard character of

125

Bohun, the Q.C., is manipulated that Shaw succeeds in making the last act just as lively as those that precede it. Bohun makes a spectacular entrance dressed in a false nose and a domino, and is described in a stage direction as 'a grotesquely majestic stranger'. He is 'imposing and disquieting', with a 'powerful menacing voice' and 'strong inexorable manner' (Act Four CP 209). His opening words are direct and uncompromising, and produce an effect of awe in his listeners—'My name is Bohun'. He dominates the scene from the moment of his entrance, an impression that is reinforced by the way in which he treats William, the waiter, and the manner in which William reacts to him when he realises that Bohun is his own son. The lawyer betrays no family feeling for his father, but concentrates on the matter in hand, while William loses all self-possession when faced with his son in a professional capacity. The effect is to isolate Bohun even further from the other characters. He occupies the central position on the stage, the fancy dress he wears when entering sets him apart from the others who are all wearing evening dress, and his apparent freedom from ties of affection lends him a superhuman air. The stage is set for a commanding performance by this imposing figure.

It is only when we have finished reading or watching the play that we realise how Shaw has hoodwinked us. He allows Bohun to override all objections from the other characters on stage, and has Dolly Clandon voice the reactions of them all when she says to Bohun: 'Oh, dear, you *are* a regular overwhelmer! Do you always go on like this?' (CP 213). The lawyer's arrogance is startling, he interrupts characters when they are in the middle of explanations, and states with certainty: 'My speciality is being right when other people are wrong' (CP 211). Shaw gives him a repetitive speech pattern which allows no retort from the person addressed, as can be seen from the following examples:

BOHUN: Now, Mr Crampton, the facts are before you: both of them. You think youd like to have your two youngest children to live with you. Well, you wouldnt—(CRAMPTON *tries to protest; but* BOHUN *will not have it on any terms*) no you wouldnt: you think you would; but I know better than you. . . .　　　　　ACT FOUR CP 213

Later, Bohun's domineering way can be seen in an exchange with Gloria, Mrs. Clandon's elder daughter:

BOHUN: The other lady intends to get married.
GLORIA (*flushing*): Mr Bohun!
BOHUN: Oh yes you do: you dont know it; but you do.

ACT FOUR CP 214

Near the end of the play the same trick of speech is again very evident:

VALENTINE: My good sir, I dont want advice for myself. Give *her* some advice.
BOHUN: She wont take it. When youre married, she wont take yours either—(*turning suddenly on* GLORIA) oh no you wont: you think you will; but you wont. He'll set to work and earn his living—(*turning suddenly on* VALENTINE) oh yes you will: you think you wont; but you will. She'll make you.

ACT FOUR CP 217

The use of punctuation adds to the effect Shaw is aiming for. The colons and semi-colons break up the sentences into short, sharp clauses that Bohun can rattle off at his listeners, but within the individual clause (such as 'Oh yes you do') punctuation is non-existent, to encourage the actor to utter the words rapidly and achieve the greatest effect.

What William, the waiter, in the last speech of the play, calls his son's 'commanding and masterful disposition' is also emphasised by the way in which the character moves on stage. We have seen in the last speech quoted above how he 'turns suddenly' on Gloria and then on Valentine. The histrionic aspect of the lawyer is stressed throughout the scene, with Bohun 'placing himself magisterially in the middle of the group' (CP 210) and from time to time throwing himself back in the chair to listen to the grievances of the other characters. He is forever pouncing forward or waving away objections imperiously; in fact, he is a caricature of all the stage barristers one has ever seen.

Bohun's visit has succeeded in cutting through most of the problems connected with Mrs. Clandon's children. His common sense, cloaked beneath his exaggerated manner, has pointed out the futility of Crampton's going to law about them. Bohun has proved to be something of a magician, as might have been expected on the night of a fancy dress ball. Shaw reinforces the point when he has him take up his domino and false nose once more and writes that he 'is again grotesquely transfigured'. Dolly, the only person in the play who has really stood up to him, and that, significantly, by echoing his own speech mannerisms, is the one to realise that the magician has put away his instruments. Seeing him in fancy dress, she runs to him, and says:

DOLLY: Oh, now you look quite like a human being. Maynt I have just one dance with you? *Can* you dance? ACT FOUR CP 214

Bohun's reply is reminiscent of his forceful statements throughout the act:

BOHUN (*thunderously*): Yes: you think I cant; but I can. Allow me.
ACT FOUR CP 214

The speed at which Bohun's decisions are taken in Act Four of *You Never Can Tell*, combined with the fact that he interrupts the other characters at will and causes them to be in awe of him, makes the audience or reader feel satisfied by the way Shaw has presented him while he is on stage. The author has used a common theatrical technique, that of making the reactions of the other characters represent the reactions of his audience. The characters are amazed and put down, so the members of the audience feel that in the same situation they would have been. The character of Bohun is not three-dimensional, but as a stage figure he is satisfactory. The play requires a boost in the final act, and Shaw's control of stagecraft and knowledge of what constitutes theatrical effectiveness enables him to know that Bohun will pass muster while the audience is in the theatre, and that is all that is required in a play of this nature.

DOOLITTLE

A somewhat similar case to that of Bohun exists in *Pygmalion* in the character of Doolittle, the dustman. He appears in only two of the play's scenes and occupies a central place in each, without ever convincing the audience or reader of his 'reality'. We are content to accept him on the stage while realising that it is extremely unlikely that a dustman would have such command of language and logic. Doolittle's function in the play has been discussed more fully in Chapter 6. It is only necessary here to point out the parallels between his appearance in the last act of *Pygmalion* and Bohun's arrival on the scene in *You Never Can Tell*. Both characters are introduced (or re-introduced in the case of Doolittle) at a point in the play where a new burst of vitality is needed; each character has a somewhat outrageous way of speaking which captures the audience's attention at once; each is dressed in an unusual way, Bohun in mask and cloak, Doolittle, the dustman, in resplendent morning clothes. The reactions of Bohun and Doolittle to the situations in which they find themselves are extremely unconventional; Bohun is rude, domineering and will brook no opposition, while Doolittle, recipient of a fortune from the Wannafeller Moral Reform League, sees himself finally defeated by middle-class morality and enters upon marriage with a heavy heart, telling his hearers that the woman with whom he has lived for years has 'been very low, thinking of the happy days that are no more' (Act Five CP 748). It will be seen that Bohun and Doolittle are exaggerated characters who achieve what their creator wants them to achieve—they add vitality to their plays at an important point, structurally speaking, but no reader or spectator could claim that they are 'real' people.

STAGE 'TYPES'

Before considering Shaw's treatment of women in his plays, and the occasions when he was really able to delve deeply into character to create a memorable, universal figure like Saint Joan or Captain Shotover, it is worth drawing attention to the way in which he was often willing to create *types* as characters in his plays. Sometimes the use of types was dictated by the theatrical form in which he had chosen to write. For example, at various stages in his career Shaw wrote plays burlesquing politics. In two short plays written during the First World War, *O'Flaherty, V.C.* (1915) and *Augustus Does His Bit* (1916), rather crude satire on the military mind is his aim. General Sir Pearce Madigan in

O'Flaherty, V.C. is the typical English landowner in Ireland, while in the latter play the vacuous Lord Augustus Highcastle is very much the 'silly ass' from the old boy network placed in a position of command merely because of his aristocratic connections. In the two plays deep characterisation would be out of place when Shaw is aiming to make his impact quickly through situation. Nevertheless, he does manage to give some individuality to the character of O'Flaherty himself, who has one moving speech about the realities of war which is a point of stillness and reflection in the midst of the exaggeratedly comic Irish happenings of the play.

o'flaherty: Ive learnt more than youd think, sir; for how would a
    gentleman like you know what a poor ignorant conceited creature
    I was when I went from here into the wide world as a soldier? What
    use is all the lying, and pretending, and humbugging, and letting
    on, when the day comes to you that your comrade is killed in the
    trench beside you, and you dont as much as look round at him until
    you trip over his poor body, and then all you say is to ask why the
    hell the stretcher-bearers dont take it out of the way.... CP 822

In other plays Shaw uses political types for satirical effect and sometimes he even goes so far as to place recognisable caricatures of real politicians on stage. In *The Apple Cart* several of the members of the cabinet are little more than cartoon figures, particularly Bill Boanerges, the trade union leader, whereas an earlier play, *Press Cuttings* (1909), was refused a licence by the Lord Chamberlain since it contained two characters, General Mitchener and the Prime Minister, Balsquith, who were obviously intended to recall aspects of General Kitchener and the politicians Asquith and Balfour. In these instances, Shaw's overall intention in writing the play did not call for characterisation of any depth. Instant recognition of the real personalities behind the stage figures was all that he asked for.

It is always necessary to look for Shaw's aim in writing a particular play before coming to a decision about the effectiveness of his characterisation. In Captain Shotover, Hector and Hesione Hushabye, and Saint Joan, to name only a few, he has succeeded in creating individual characters with a sense of depth. However, even within *Heartbreak House* and *Saint Joan* there are various levels of delineation of character, as can be seen from a consideration of *Saint Joan*. Shaw's intention in the play was to isolate Joan, to show how she differed from those with whom she came in contact; to show, in short, what made her a saint. Therefore, apart from Joan herself, most of the other characters in the play are portrayed as types. These are the blustering captain, the downtrodden steward, the archbishop, the jingoistic de Stogumber, the Inquisitor. All of these characters are chiefly important, not as individuals, but for the functions they perform. The spotlight is therefore directed more brightly upon Joan herself and attention is not drawn away from her by having equally interesting and developed individuals to share the stage with her. Even the Dauphin and Warwick seem to exist *because* of Joan; their actions and reactions are only interesting to us because of how they affect her.

CHARACTERISATION IN THE LATER PLAYS

After the production of *The Apple Cart*, which ran for 258 performances in London in 1929–30, Shaw had only one more commercial success with a new play in his lifetime. *Geneva* had 237 performances in London in 1938–9. During the 'thirties he wrote six full-length plays, of which four were given London productions. Except for *Geneva*, the longest run was that of *Too True to be Good* which was performed forty-seven times in 1932. It would be wrong to equate artistic quality with commercial success, but it is hard to avoid the conclusion that Shaw's concentration on the communication of ideas without caring too much for their effective presentation in dramatic terms was largely responsible for the failure to achieve a long West End run. The relative failure of the plays written in the 'thirties can be partly attributed to the lack of attention to characterisation.

Village Wooing, written in 1933, is an amusing trifle, consisting of three conversations between a man and a woman. In the course of these conversations Shaw's unusual views on marriage are once more given an airing. What is interesting is to see the way in which concentration on the argument has taken over entirely from care paid to characterisation, as it had threatened to do in the debate-drama of *The Apple Cart*. What is said is much more important than who is saying it, and it would not be too fanciful to assume that Shaw's designation of his characters as 'A' and 'Z' serves to indicate his lack of interest in them as individuals.

'TOO TRUE TO BE GOOD'

Too True to be Good (1931) is chiefly interesting for two reasons; one of its characters is not human, and another is based upon a famous friend of Shaw's. One of the themes of the play is Shaw's belief that most of the ills of humanity are caused by over-indulgence. It begins in the sick-room of a rich young woman who is suffering from measles. After an attempt by her dishonest nurse and a burglar to steal her jewels, she decides to join them in their disreputable life, and the excitement of deciding to do something that she really wants to do cures her. Shaw enters the realms of fantasy in the first act of the play by having a measles microbe on stage: 'Near her, in the easy chair, sits a Monster. In shape and size it resembles a human being; but in substance it seems to be made of a luminous jelly with a visible skeleton of short black rods. It droops forward in the chair with its head in its hands, and seems in the last degree wretched' (Act One CP 1132).

Part of the humour of the act is a result of the Monster's reactions to the doctor and the disease from which the patient is suffering. The Monster blames the patient for giving *him* the disease: 'Measles! German measles! And she's given them to me, a poor innocent microbe that never did her any harm. And she says that *I* gave them to her. Oh, is this justice?' (CP 1132).

The fact that Shaw asks the audience to accept that the Monster's remarks cannot be heard by some of the other characters on stage increases the humour. It is a common device; the invisible man situation has often been used by other authors, such as H. G. Wells, in *The Invisible Man* (1897) and Shakespeare, who allows Puck to be invisible (and unheard by the lovers) in *A Midsummer Night's Dream*.

At the end of the act the Monster is used by Shaw to make a combative reference to the way that the play is going to develop:

THE MONSTER: The play is now virtually over; but the characters will discuss it at great length for two acts more. The exit doors are all in order.   ACT ONE CP 1141

Among the characters who continue to 'discuss it at great length' is Private Meek, although, to be fair to Shaw, he is chiefly observed acting rather than talking. In the stage directions we are told that 'He is an insignificant looking private soldier, dusty as to his clothes and a bit gritty as to his windbeaten face' (Act Two CP 1141). He rides 'a powerful and very imperfectly silenced motor bicycle', and at the end of Act Two, when he has shown great military initiative in warding off an attack by hostile tribesmen, we learn that, whereas he was once a colonel, he has voluntarily relinquished the rank:

TALLBOYS: And how do you come to be a private now?
MEEK: I prefer the ranks, sir. I have a freer hand. And the conversation in the officers' mess doesnt suit me. I always resign a commission and enlist again.
TALLBOYS: Always! How many commissions have you held?
MEEK: I dont quite remember, sir. Three, I think.
        ACT TWO CP 1153-1154

Quite obviously, Meek is a portrait of Shaw's friend, T. E. Lawrence (Lawrence of Arabia). Lawrence was an unconventional military leader, and, as we know from his book *The Mint*, spurned the fame that was his due after the First World War to join the R.A.F. as an ordinary aircraftman, taking as his pseudonym T. E. Shaw. Bernard Shaw and his wife gave him a powerful motorcycle as a present, and it was while riding this machine that he was killed. To play the part of Meek in the first production of *Too True to be Good*, Shaw chose the actor Walter Hudd, who bore a striking resemblance to Lawrence, so that the parallel could hardly be missed by anyone attending the play. Even the introduction of a portrait of one of his friends into a play was not a new departure for Shaw, however. Miss Blanche Patch, Shaw's secretary, in her book, *Thirty Years With G.B.S.* (1951),

133

reminds us that in *Arms and the Man*, Sidney Webb, one of the founders of the Fabian Society, figures as an inn-keeper, and that Gilbert Murray, the professor of Greek, and Henry Sweet, the phonetician, are the models for Cusins in *Major Barbara* and Higgins in *Pygmalion*.

POLITICAL FIGURES IN 'GENEVA'

As I noted earlier, Shaw's last commercial success in the theatre with a new play, in his lifetime, was achieved by *Geneva*, which ran for 237 performances in London, after being presented at the Malvern Festival in August 1938. In this play Shaw reverts to the manner of characterisation which he used in presenting the political types in *Press Cuttings*. In the characters of Battler, Bombardone and Sir Orpheus Midlander he portrays the dictators, Hitler and Mussolini, and the English Prime Minister, Neville Chamberlain. The Spanish dictator, Franco, also appears as General Flanco de Fortinbras.

It is well known that Shaw was attracted by totalitarianism in its various manifestations during the nineteen-thirties. This partly explains his admiration for Russian Communism as practised under Stalin, but one is forced to the conclusion that like many law-abiding intellectuals Shaw was impressed by the forceful personalities of Stalin, Hitler and Mussolini, in spite of the policies they were advocating. We should not forget that he had always admired the writings of the German philosopher, Friedrich Nietzsche (1844–1900), populariser of the doctrine of the Superman, and it was on a perversion of Nietzsche's ideas that the Nazis based their case for the creation of a master race.

From the Preface to *Geneva*, which was written seven years later than the play itself, and published after the war, it is evident that Shaw has become discriminating about Hitler and Mussolini. He describes Hitler as having magnetism, and being a 'national benefactor who began by abolishing unemployment, tearing up the Treaty of Versailles, and restoring the selfrespect of sixty millions of his fellow countrymen' (CPBS 882), but he goes on to say that he 'became the mad Messiah who, as lord of a Chosen Race, was destined to establish the Kingdom of God on earth—a

German Kingdom of a German God—by military conquest of the rest of mankind' (CPBS 882). He writes more warmly of Mussolini.

In the play itself, the characters are allowed to present their points of view concerning government, treatment of the Jews and other political questions. Hitler's noted sentimentality, which contrasted so vividly with his attitude towards those he conquered, is brought out towards the end of the play. News has arrived at the International Court, in which the play takes place, that the earth is jumping to a wider orbit, taking it millions of miles away from the sun.

SECRETARY: The icecaps that we have on the north and south poles will spread over the whole earth. Even the polar bears will be frozen stiff. Not a trace of any sort of life known to us will be possible on this earth. ACT FOUR CP 1331–2

Bombardone is appalled to see Battler in tears:

BOMBARDONE: You also, Ernest, must—What! Crying!! For shame, man! The world looks to us for leadership. Shall it find us in tears?

Battler's reply is:

'Let me alone. My dog Blonda will be frozen to death. My doggie! My little doggie! (*He breaks down, sobbing convulsively*).' ACT FOUR CP 1332

It is on such caricature that the play depends for much of its interest. However, the dictators are allowed their say, particularly on their methods of rousing mobs by public oratory, and their speeches contain some sound observation:

BATTLER: We all begin as understudies, and end, perhaps, as great actors. The army was a school in which I learnt a good deal, because whoever has my capacity for learning can learn something even in the worst school. The army is the worst school, because fighting is not a whole-time-job, and in the army they pretend that it is. It ends in the discharged soldier being good for nothing until he recovers his civilian sense and the habit of thinking for himself. . . . ACT FOUR CP 1322

Shaw has stated that he has allowed the dictators to put forward their ideas freely. While *Geneva* was running he made several revisions to fit changes in the political situation, and thus the play had a topicality that accounted for much of its interest. In recent years we have seen plays such as *The Representative* and *Soldiers*, by Rolf Hochhuth, achieve prominence because they portray actual persons from recent history, such as Pope Pius XII and Winston Churchill, under their own names. In 1938 theatrical censorship would not allow such open dealing, but the success of *Geneva* was obviously the result of the public's curiosity to see 'Hitler' and 'Mussolini' on stage. The play has never been revived in London, which suggests that its now dated topicality outweighs interest in its construction and characterisation.

WOMEN

If we think of Shaw's dramatic output we cannot fail to be struck by the prominence which he gave to female characters in his plays. In other chapters the importance of Mrs. Warren, Major Barbara, Eliza Doolittle, and Mrs. Hushabye, to name only four, has been commented on. A few words about his attitude to women in the plays may be appropriate here.

While recognising the dangers of biographical criticism, it is hard to avoid the feeling that Shaw was reflecting his own complexes concerning women when writing about them, as well as carrying out his aim of putting the Ibsenite 'New Woman' on the stage. We have noted elsewhere his admiration for the dominant woman in such characters as Ann Whitefield, Saint Joan and Vivie Warren. It is there, too, in the way that he presents Lina Szczepanowska, the Polish acrobat in *Misalliance* (1909–10), and even Epifania in *The Millionairess* (1935), and we should not overlook the fact that he portrays women as political leaders in *The Apple Cart* (1929), the play which contains the terrifying portrait of Orinthia, the King's mistress.

It would seem that Shaw was attracted by the idea of the all-powerful woman both for intellectual and subjective reasons. In the treatment of Epifania, the central character of *The Million-*

airess, there is a liveliness which does not extend to any other character in the play. Once again Shaw's obsession that women embody the vitality of the race is aired. Epifania far outshines the male characters in vitality and magnetism, even if that does not in itself make *The Millionairess* a good play. This is a theme that Shaw has emphasised throughout his career, and is based on his belief that women are the predators and instigators of all that is progressive in society. Mrs. Warren, Ann Whitefield, Gloria Clandon, Cleopatra and Hesione Hushabye all have this in common—they possess a fantastic energy, and it is this which Shaw feels will ensure the survival and development of the human race. It is significant that he causes Lilith, the embodiment of the female principle, to speak the final words of *Back to Methuselah* (1918–1920), the play into which he put the summation of his philosophical views. The speech is too long to quote in full.

LILITH: And though all that they have done seems but the first hour of the infinite work of creation, yet I will not supersede them until they have forded this last stream that lies between flesh and spirit, and disentangled their life from the matter that has always mocked it. I can wait: waiting and patience mean nothing to the eternal. I gave the woman the greatest of gifts: curiosity. By that her seed has been saved from my wrath; for I also am curious; and I have waited always to see what they will do tomorrow. Let them feed that appetite well for me. I say, let them dread, of all things, stagnation . . .   PART FIVE CP 962

So the dominant woman attracted Shaw and appears in many of his plays. Often, however, she is counterbalanced by a cosy, maternal figure, to whom the hero turns for comfort when the dominance becomes too wearing. In *The Apple Cart* Magnus evades the charms of Orinthia, his glamorous mistress, to go to tea with his wife. In *In Good King Charles's Golden Days* the final scene shows Charles II in his wife's room, seeking peace away from the mistresses we have seen him with earlier. It is a tender but somewhat over-sentimental scene, and the pain behind some of Catherine of Braganza's comments can be felt. It is difficult not to think of Shaw's private life when one is reading these scenes. We know that he was extremely attracted towards Ellen Terry and Mrs. Patrick Campbell, two of the most famous actresses during his time in the theatre, although he preferred the idea of being in love to actually doing anything about it. The scenes in *The Apple Cart* and *In Good King Charles's Golden Days* are a working out of Shaw's own position; he was attracted to the brilliant actresses, but preferred always to return to the sexless (perhaps maternal) safety of Mrs. Shaw.

In this chapter I have tried to show how the reader or member of the audience must always try to make himself aware of Shaw's aims in a particular play before coming to a conclusion as to the effectiveness of his characterisation. Usually he will find that Shaw's characterisation is suitable to his purpose; if the play demands an artificial boost he provides it; if political caricature is all that is required then he is content to write in that way. He is an author who is at home in many moods, and, in other chapters, we have seen his capacity to create living, three-dimensional figures. Towards the end of his career characterisation tended to interest him less than did the use of the theatre as a platform for public debate, but it seems likely that the plays for which he will be remembered longest are those where he paid most attention to theatrical qualities, and those include the creation of memorable characters such as Caesar, William the waiter and Saint Joan.

7

The Prose Writings

Although I have been chiefly concerned in this book with Shaw as a playwright, it would be wrong to overlook his non-dramatic writings. They are distinguished by the great variety of their subject-matter, but almost from the beginning Shaw established an individual voice in his writing. Whether he is working on dramatic criticism, a preface to a play, or a book concerned with political theory, the style is unmistakably his own. He falls naturally into a one-to-one relationship with his readers, so that they feel involved in an interchange of views with the author. Thus in all his prose works the presence of the *dramatist* can be sensed.

Shaw began his literary career as a novelist, but had great difficulty in getting any of his novels published. The Americans brought them out in 'pirate' editions (without paying the author a fee), but Shaw's lack of success in this field of writing is shown by the fact that English royalties on the books amounted to only seven and tenpence for the year 1891. Nevertheless, Shaw was always glad that he had worked on the novels before becoming a playwright, as he believed that the experience gained in writing them taught him the author's craft.

After becoming established as a dramatist, he returned to writing ordinary prose works at intervals throughout his career. His over-riding interest in political matters led to his writing *The Intelligent Woman's Guide to Socialism*, which was published in 1928, and *Everybody's Political What's What*, published in 1944. The former work began as a leaflet written to help his sister-in-law to explain Socialism to her branch of the Women's Institute, but developed into a 200,000-word book; while Shaw spent most of the Second World War writing *Everybody's Political What's What*.

He was, however, capable of writing shorter prose works. Just as he sometimes felt the need to relax from the efforts of writing full-length plays, and produce a twenty-minute trifle such as *Annajanska, the Bolshevik Empress*, so he occasionally wrote a short story merely to keep his hand in. His most successful attempt is *The Black Girl in Search of God*, an allegorical tale concerning the origins of religious controversy. In the Preface Shaw writes:

> I was inspired to write this tale when I was held up in Knysna for five weeks in the African summer and English winter of 1932. My intention was to write a play in the ordinary course of my business as a playwright; but I found myself writing the story of the black girl instead.   CPBS 645

In the story Shaw follows a literary line that goes back to Voltaire's *Candide* and Swift's *Gulliver's Travels*. In both of these books a seeming innocent is placed in strange environments and the authors are able to comment satirically on those environments by showing the ways in which their heroes react to them. *The Black Girl in Search of God* begins with the heroine asking her missionary teacher, 'Where is God?' Receiving the reply, 'He has said "Seek and ye shall find me" ', she takes it literally and strides off into the forest to find Him, armed with her bible and knobkerry. In the course of her journey the black girl meets many characters whom she questions in a seemingly naïve way concerning God's whereabouts. By means of these encounters and the black girl's reactions, Shaw is able to examine religious belief in its many aspects. Early in the tale Shaw tells us 'instead of taking Christianity with sweet docility exactly as it was administered to her, she met it with unexpected interrogative reactions which forced her teacher to improvise doctrinal replies and invent evidence on the spur of the moment'. The character is well-drawn for his purpose, and the encounters wittily illustrate the points he wishes to make.

The debt the story owes to *Candide* in structure and moral is reinforced towards the end when the black girl meets an old gentleman: 'Nothing particular happened after that until she came to a prim little villa with a very amateurish garden which was being cultivated by a wizened old gentleman whose eyes were so striking that his face seemed all eyes, his nose so remarkable that his face seemed all nose, and his mouth so expressive of a comically malicious relish that his face seemed all mouth until the black girl combined these three incompatibles by deciding that his face was all intelligence.' The fact that the garden is being cultivated tells the reader immediately that the old gentleman is Voltaire, since in *Candide* the hero decides, after a life of terrible misadventures, that he and his wife and friends must work in their garden, having been told by a Turkish patriarch that agricultural 'work banishes those three great evils, boredom, vice, and poverty'. The old gentleman in Shaw's story tells the black girl, 'I have found, after a good deal of consideration, that the best place to seek God is in a garden. You can dig for Him here.'

The old gentleman's summing up of his beliefs reminds the reader of the doctrine to be found in many of Shaw's plays, particularly *Back to Methuselah*; that man must work hard and feel himself to be fully used if he is to develop in the future:

> 'And shall we never be able to bear His full presence?' said the black girl.
> 'I trust not' said the old philosopher. 'For we shall never be able to bear His full presence until we have fulfilled all His purposes and becomes gods ourselves.'

This idea is hinted at in Part One of *Back to Methuselah*, when Adam says:

> 'I like you; but I do not like myself. I want to be different; to be better; to begin again and again; to shed myself as a snake sheds its skin.' PART ONE ACT ONE CP 856

The sense one receives of physical activity when Adam speaks of 'shedding' himself is important. One cannot improve oneself by remaining passive, and the point is reinforced by Eve's final speech in Part One Act Two:

> 'Man need not always live by bread alone. There is something
> else. We do not yet know what it is; but some day we shall find out;
> and then we will live on that alone; and there shall be no more
> digging nor spinning, nor fighting nor killing.'   CP 869

Over-simplified, the old philosopher's message in *The Black
Girl in Search of God* could be said to be the same as that of
Shaw's social plays, including *Mrs. Warren's Profession* and *Major
Barbara*: bread must come before philosophy; physical conditions
must be improved before man can be interested in abstract
questions. The old philosopher implies that work must be done,
and, by solving the problems it poses, man will come to understand God. Typically, Shaw does not leave it at that. The black
girl's final encounter is with a red-haired Irishman, who tells her
he is a Socialist. He is sceptical about God:

> 'My own belief is that he's not all that he sets up to be. He's not
> properly made and finished yet. Theres somethin in us thats dhrivin
> at him, and somethin out of us thats dhrivin at him: thats certain;
> and the only other thing thats certain is that the somethin makes
> plenty of mistakes in thryin to get there. We'v got to find out its
> way for it as best we can, you and I; for theres a hell of a lot of other
> people thinkin of nothin but their own bellies.'

The Irishman is, of course, Shaw himself. The black girl
marries him against his will, and raises a family, and, we are told,
'was kept so busy that her search for God was crowded out of her
head most of the time'.

The story is witty and effective, without reaching the levels
of profundity to be found in the best of the plays. It is dramatic
in tone, with extremely speakable dialogue, so it is not surprising
that in 1967 it was adapted for the stage by Basil Ashmore and
produced at the Mermaid Theatre in London.

THE PREFACES

The short stories and the political treatises are not the prose
works by which Shaw will be remembered, however. His
reputation as a writer of non-dramatic prose will rest on the
Prefaces to the plays, and on his criticism. The two-fold origin
of the Prefaces is interesting.

In the first chapter I explained that Shaw had difficulty in establishing himself as a dramatist, just as he had earlier experienced little success with his novels. Like Ibsen before him, he had to rely for a large proportion of his income from the early plays on the reading public. Accordingly, he paid a lot of attention to describing the settings and the characters of his plays, almost as a novelist might do. He went further, however, as he described in a statement to Hesketh Pearson, who reproduces it in his biography of Shaw:

> 'I always considered that books should be sold by weight, like Government blue books, at so much the ounce,' he said to me, 'and as I wanted my books to take a long time in going round the family, I determined to give full value for money.'

This determination led to the inclusion of a Preface or Prefaces with each volume of plays published. Sometimes the Preface is longer than the printed text of the actual play, so that *Androcles and the Lion* in the Penguin edition, for example, contains ninety-eight pages of Preface to forty-four pages of play.

Apart from the commercial reason for writing the Prefaces there was another, more important, motive. Shaw was inexhaustible, and he could always find more to say about any subject that interested him than he could include in a play. In the Introduction to *The Complete Prefaces of Bernard Shaw*, he writes:

> You may well ask me why . . . I took the trouble to write them. I can only reply that I do not know. There was no why about it: I had to: that was all. CPBS viii

In the same introduction Shaw reminds his readers that most of the Prefaces 'were written long after the plays to which they are attached had been repeatedly performed'. Miss Blanche Patch, Shaw's secretary, in *Thirty Years With G.B.S.*, writes:

> His prefaces, as he explained to one playgoer, were essays, quite independent of the plays, written when their subject was too large to be fully dealt with on the stage; and it was nonsense to think that they were meant for playgoers to read before the plays could be understood.

It is true, up to a point, that the Prefaces are independent of the plays. That is to say that the plays can usually be understood and enjoyed without knowing the Prefaces, but a reading of the latter will always enhance the pleasure a reader can obtain from the plays. The Prefaces cover a great variety of subject matter, but fall into two main categories:

I Theatrical and autobiographical.

II Argumentative and controversial.

These categories are by no means exclusive, but in general it is true to say that in the early Prefaces Shaw directs his attention to 'placing' the play for the reader, while when he became an established dramatist he felt free to continue the philosophical arguments of the plays in the Prefaces that precede them in their printed versions.

I Theatrical and Autobiographical

In the Prefaces to *Plays Unpleasant* (1898), *Plays Pleasant* (1898), and parts of that to *Three Plays for Puritans* (1901), Shaw is concerned with explaining to his readers the theatrical conditions under which his early plays came to be written and produced. We also learn from them a great deal about how he saw his own development as a writer.

The Preface to *Plays Unpleasant* is typical of those he wrote in this early period. It contains a full account of the genesis of *Widowers' Houses* and *Mrs. Warren's Profession*, and is written in the exaggeratedly emphatic style with which Shaw's readers were to become familiar. Describing the reception of *Widowers' Houses*, he writes, 'It made a sensation out of all proportion to its merits or even its demerits; and I at once became infamous as a playwright' (CPBS 719). The love of paradox that was to be associated with Shaw for the rest of his writing life is there in that sentence with its 'infamous'. Not only did the play stand usually accepted conventions on their heads, but the Preface continues the process.

This Preface is chiefly important for its account of the way in which the presence of the Lord Chamberlain's Examiner prevented the production of *Mrs. Warren's Profession*. Many playwrights since Shaw's day have written against the system of censorship of plays that existed in England from the 18th century until 1968, but few have made the existence of the Examiner's powers seem so ridiculous and unjust as Shaw does here:

> The robbery takes the form of making me pay him two guineas for reading every play of mine that exceeds one act in length. I do not want him to read it (at least officially: personally he is welcome): on the contrary, I strenuously resent that impertinence on his part. But I must submit in order to obtain from him an insolent and insufferable document, which I cannot read without boiling of the blood, certifying that in his opinion—*his* opinion!—my play 'does not in its general tendency contain anything immoral or otherwise improper for the stage,' and that the Lord Chamberlain therefore 'allows' its performance (confound his impudence!).   CPBS 720

Shaw goes on to describe how he prepared his plays for publication, a subject that has been touched on elsewhere. It is hard to tell whether he is being wholly serious when he censures Shakespeare in the course of this discussion. He wishes that Shakespeare had provided 'descriptive directions' and 'above all, the character sketches, however brief, by which he tried to convey to the actor the sort of person he meant him to incarnate' (CPBS 724). Many of us, while finding Shaw's own descriptions of, say, the steward in *Saint Joan* witty and memorable—'a trodden worm, scanty of flesh, scanty of hair, who might be any age from 18 to 55, being the sort of man whom age cannot wither because he has never bloomed' (Scene One CP 963)—feel that so often the directions are impossible for an actor to convey to an audience, and find it hard to regret that Shakespeare left his texts as he did.

In spite of the care that he took over the printing of his plays, it is quite clear that Shaw would never have been content to remain an unperformed playwright. In 1902 he added a separate Preface to *Mrs. Warren's Profession*, which had recently been performed in a so-called club performance by the Stage Society. (During the 20th century many plays unacceptable to the Lord Chamberlain have been produced in club theatres and performed to audiences whose members have each paid a nominal fee to join the club. Among plays by reputable authors to have been produced in this way are *Cat on a Hot Tin Roof* by Tennessee Williams and *A Patriot For Me* by John Osborne.) In Shaw's Preface he states ironically:

> *Mrs Warren's Profession* has been performed at last, after a delay of only eight years; and I have once more shared with Ibsen the triumphant amusement of startling all but the strongest-headed of the London theatre critics clean out of the practice of their profession. CPBS 220

The Preface is a splendid defence of the morality of the play, and of the use of drama as a means of improving society:

> That is why I fight the theatre, not with pamphlets and sermons and treatises, but with plays; and so effective do I find the dramatic method that I have no doubt I shall at last persuade even London to take its conscience and its brains with it when it goes to the theatre, instead of leaving them at home with its prayer-book as it does at present. CPBS 221

It is important to note that Shaw speaks here of finding 'the dramatic method' effective, and writes of 'London taking its conscience and its brains . . . to the *theatre*'. No matter how often he decries the powers of actors to act intelligently or audiences to understand fully, he is always conscious that it is in the theatre that his plays will make most impact.

The Preface to *Plays Pleasant* is mainly about things theatrical. He begins by describing the commercial success (or lack of it) experienced with *Arms and the Man* and continues with comments on the writing of *The Man of Destiny* and *You Never Can Tell*. Elsewhere in this book I have mentioned that Shaw did nothing in his early works to extend thinking about dramatic form and here, in this Preface, he confirms this point:

> *You Never Can Tell* was an attempt to comply with many requests for a play in which the much paragraphed 'brilliancy' of *Arms and the Man* should be tempered by some consideration for the requirements of managers in search of fashionable comedies for West End theatres. I had no difficulty in complying, as I have always cast my plays in the ordinary practical comedy form in use at all the theatres; CPBS 730

We are reminded of this passage when we come to read the Preface to *Three Plays for Puritans*. There Shaw goes further in his denial of novelty of technique. Just as he has told us that *You Never Can Tell* is based on a popular dramatic form, so we learn of *The Devil's Disciple* that 'It does not contain a single even passably novel incident. Every old patron of the Adelphi pit would, were he not beglamored in a way presently to be explained, recognize the reading of the will, the oppressed orphan finding a protector, the arrest, the heroic sacrifice, the court martial, the scaffold, the reprieve at the last moment, as he recognizes beefsteak pudding on the bill of fare at his restaurant' (CPBS 745).

Returning to *Plays Pleasant* we find that Shaw is chiefly concerned in the remainder of his Preface with the difficulties of production in the commercial theatre, in the process throwing off one or two illuminating comments about his own writing and beliefs:

> When a comedy is performed, it is nothing to me that the spectators laugh: any fool can make an audience laugh. I want to see how many of them, laughing or grave, are in the melting mood.
>
> CPBS 733
>
> ... idealism, which is only a flattering name for romance in politics and morals, is as obnoxious to me as romance in ethics or religion.   CPBS 734

The Prefaces to *Plays Unpleasant* and *Plays Pleasant* contain enough that is controversial and paradoxical for us to see the Shaw of the later Prefaces in them, but they are chiefly of importance in helping the reader to understand the theatrical climate in which the plays contained in the two volumes were written. The Preface to *Three Plays For Puritans* marks the point of transition from those Prefaces which deal with theatrical background to the later polemical Prefaces.

In the section 'On Diabolonian Ethics' Shaw puts up a spirited defence of the practice of writing Prefaces. The tone is challenging from the outset:

> There is a foolish opinion prevalent that an author should allow his works to speak for themselves, and that he who appends and

> prefixes explanations to them is likely to be as bad an artist as the
> painter cited by Cervantes, who wrote under his picture This is a
> Cock, lest there should be any mistake about it.   CPBS 744

In the course of his defence, Shaw develops further the argument
about Shakespeare's plays that he began in the Preface to *Plays
Unpleasant*. There, while allowing Shakespeare's pre-eminence,
he writes of Shakespeare's having 'left us no intellectually
coherent drama' (CPBS 724), and says that this is because he did
not have to prepare his plays for publication in competition with
fiction as elaborate as that of Meredith. In the Preface to *Three
Plays For Puritans* he is even more provocative:

> I write prefaces as Dryden did, and treatises as Wagner, because I
> *can*; and I would give half a dozen of Shakespear's plays for one of
> the prefaces he ought to have written.   CPBS 745

The Preface is a mixture of theatrical background information,
self-advertisement and philosophical argument on such matters as
the nature of the greatness of a person like Julius Caesar. We have
already looked at Shaw's statement that *The Devil's Disciple* is a
rehash of all the plots of the old melodramas. Shaw goes on to
deny originality in anything but *treatment* of events and ideas:

> Now this, if it applies to the incidents, plot, construction, and
> general professional and technical qualities of the play, is nonsense;
> for the truth is, I am in these matters a very old-fashioned play-
> wright.   CPBS 745

Old-fashioned playwright or not, in the Preface to *Three Plays
For Puritans* he is taking a great step forward. While still giving
the reader the impression of taking him into his confidence by
telling him all kinds of seemingly intimate details ('I am a natural-
born mountebank.' 'I have advertised myself so well that I find
myself, whilst still in middle life, almost as legendary a person
as the Flying Dutchman'), he has moved on towards polemic,
which is the ground on which most of the Prefaces will be based
from this time onwards. This is not to say that he totally abandons
autobiographical detail, or all mention of how his plays came to
be staged. Henceforth, however, the Prefaces are to be chiefly

concerned with arguments related to the subject matter of the plays.

II Argumentative and Controversial

Hesketh Pearson, in his biography of Shaw, tells us that the Prefaces cost him far more labour than the plays, and, as they expressed his personal views, he thought them more important. He is no doubt thinking of the Prefaces dealing with polemical matters when he writes this. Their variety is amazing. For example if we examine the range of subjects which form the starting points of the later Prefaces, we shall find feudalism, religion, parents and children, monarchy, medicine, evolution, money and bosses, to name only a few. The Preface to one play, *On the Rocks* (1933), even adds to the Shaw canon, containing as it does a short play in which Jesus Christ and Pontius Pilate are seen confronting one another. Incidentally, this dramatic interlude would seem to go some way to prove that Shaw was naturally drawn towards drama as a means of expressing what he felt most deeply, but discussion of the play-within-a-preface would be out of place here.

Obviously, there are too many Prefaces to deal with individually in this chapter. An examination of certain recurrent techniques that are to be found in the polemical Prefaces may be helpful, however, together with some attempt to decide how much assistance a reader would gain in his understanding of the plays if he were to read the Prefaces afterwards.

In the Prefaces attached to such plays as *The Doctor's Dilemma*, *Androcles and the Lion*, *Back to Methuselah*, and *Saint Joan*, Shaw is to be seen in the roles of teacher and preacher. He cared so deeply about the subjects with which he is dealing in these Prefaces that he wished to convince all his readers of the rightness of his own opinions concerning them. Richard M. Ohmann, in his book, *Shaw: The Style and the Man* (1962), has pointed out from an examination of Shaw's style that his chosen stance in argument is usually to appear to be in opposition to accepted points of view. We should not, therefore, be surprised to find that the tone of the Prefaces is often combative. Shaw, the street-corner orator, knew that this hard-hitting attitude can catch the attention of a listener or reader immediately. The titles of some of the early sections of the Preface to *Androcles and the Lion* indicate one way of capturing an audience—WHY NOT GIVE CHRISTIANITY A TRIAL?—WAS JESUS A COWARD?—THE GOSPELS NOW UNINTELLIGIBLE TO NOVICES. That the provocative headings served their purpose is seen by the fact that Shaw continued to use the method for the remainder of his career.

Other methods of gaining the reader's attention immediately can be seen from a glance at the opening sections of the Prefaces to *Back to Methuselah* and *Saint Joan*. Shaw must have realised that there was a danger of scaring off readers of the Preface to the former play, which deals with the doctrine of creative evolution. He therefore begins in an anecdotal, autobiographical way:

> One day early in the eighteen hundred and sixties, I, being then a small boy, was with my nurse, buying something in the shop of a petty newsagent, bookseller, and stationer in Camden Street, Dublin, when there entered an elderly man, weighty and solemn, who advanced to the counter, and said pompously, 'Have you the works of the celebrated Buffoon?'
>
> My own works were at that time unwritten, or it is possible that the shop assistant might have misunderstood me so far as to produce a copy of Man and Superman. CPBS 501

Immediately, in this rather far-fetched story about the man trying to buy the works of the famous naturalist, Buffon, Shaw has the reader on his side. The build-up is slow, with its emphasis on 'an elderly man, weighty and solemn', who spoke 'pompously', and then follows, almost as an aside, Shaw's comment about his own works. We have been interested in what I suspect is a fake dramatic situation, and Shaw has also indicated that he can laugh at himself. The Preface is off to a good start, even if what follows is sometimes heavy going.

The technique is somewhat different at the beginning of the Preface to *Saint Joan*:

> Joan of Arc, a village girl from the Vosges, was born about 1412; burnt for heresy, witchcraft, and sorcery in 1431; rehabilitated

after a fashion in 1456; designated Venerable in 1904; declared Blessed in 1908; and finally canonized in 1920. She is the most notable Warrior Saint in the Christian calendar, and the queerest fish among the eccentric worthies of the Middle Ages.   CPBS 604

Once again Shaw has gained the attention of his readers by the directness with which he begins, and in these two sentences he has given more than a hint of the ironies that his play contains, and of his own equivocal attitude towards the events it portrays. The list of verbs in the first sentence is impressive, although we can sense the worldly amusement of the author in the gradual progression towards sainthood, and we are put on our guard by the 'after a fashion' in the third section of the sentence. The antithesis of the second sentence achieves its effect with precision; the nobility of the vocabulary in the first half—'notable Warrior Saint . . . Christian calendar'—builds up expectations far different from those which are aroused by the terms 'queerest fish' and 'worthies' in the second. It would not be going too far to say that in this sentence Shaw has stated the subject-matter of his play; in *Saint Joan* what he does is to reconcile the two widely opposing points of view concerning Joan.

BREVITY OF SECTIONS

Having obtained the reader's attention, Shaw's task was to keep it. Perhaps this accounts for the way in which so many of the Prefaces are broken up into a great number of short sections, each section with its own provocative or summarising heading. It is as though Shaw realised how necessary it was to keep the argument on evolution, or Christianity, or parents and children, clear and easy to follow. It has been thought by some readers that the method also made it easy for Shaw to marshal his own thoughts. This may have been the case, but, if so, he cannot always have found it necessary, as we can see by examining the Preface to *Major Barbara*, for example, which contains only seven sections in forty-one pages in the Penguin edition. The following figures show, however, how Shaw often did find it useful or necessary to divide his Prefaces into relatively short sections of argument. (Numbers of pages refer to the Penguin editions of the respective plays.)

	No. of Sections	Pages
Androcles and the Lion	83	104
Heartbreak House	32	42
Back to Methuselah	49	63
Saint Joan	41	62

The short sections of argument that go to make up these Prefaces are always clearly linked, and we shall find, if we examine the opening sentences in the individual sections, that Shaw always begins a new stage of the argument with the air of one who is so sure that he is right that the truth of the matter must be obvious to his readers. There is no sense of needing to convince; the tone is that of a man talking about something on which all civilised people must agree. Let us look at some opening sentences from sections of the Preface to *Getting Married* (1908) and see the eminently reasonable note that Shaw adopts:

1. There is no subject on which more dangerous nonsense is talked and thought than marriage. CPBS 1
2. Now most laws are, and all laws ought to be, stronger than the strongest individual. CPBS 1
3. However much we may all suffer through marriage, most of us think so little about it that we regard it as a fixed part of the order of nature, like gravitation. CPBS 2
4. If we adopt the common romantic assumption that the object of marriage is bliss, then the very strongest reason for dissolving a marriage is that it shall be disagreeable to one or other or both of the parties. CPBS 3
5. The answer to this question is an answer which everybody knows and nobody likes to give. CPBS 4

The sense of conviction behind these firmly stated pronouncements is the first thing that strikes the reader. The next is that Shaw is drawing the reader's attention to something that is obvious to him, but not to everybody. Note the way in which Shaw assumes that 'we ... all suffer through marriage', and makes us reconsider whether the object of marriage is bliss. He also gets the reader on his side by treating him as an equal, and including him in the 'we' of sentences 3 and 4.

When we face the question of how far a reading of the Preface to a play would enable a reader to understand it more deeply we are on difficult ground. Shaw, himself, as we have seen, considered it nonsense for anyone to think that a preliminary reading of the Preface was necessary to an understanding of a play. Sometimes, however, the subject-matter of a particular play is somewhat difficult (as in the case of *Back to Methuselah*) and a knowledge of the Preface will help to simplify matters for the average reader. Perhaps the answer can only be something that an individual can give for himself. If he is ignorant of biology, a reading of the Preface to *Back to Methuselah* will make him feel more confident when reading the play; if his knowledge of the history of Joan of Arc is thin, then a reading of the Preface to *Saint Joan* will be helpful.

In general, however, I feel that the Prefaces should be read because they extend the reader's capacity to deal with new ideas, rather than because they may give him new information. We should always bear in mind that the biological doctrine or the medieval history, or whatever is the ostensible subject of the particular Preface, is always biological doctrine or medieval history, etc., *as seen by Shaw*. We read the Prefaces just as we read the plays—for the individual voice that we can hear behind the lines.

Hesketh Pearson writes in his biography of Shaw: 'There is certainly not a trace of old age in his later Prefaces'. Shaw himself was able to write in the Preface to *Farfetched Fables* (1948) of things 'troubling me in the queer second wind that follows second childhood' (CPBS 894), but what impresses most readers, even of the Prefaces written during and immediately after the Second World War, when Shaw was approaching ninety, is the continuing strength of the prose style and the openness to new ideas. He may no longer be able to sustain full-length Prefaces, or full-length plays of distinction, but they are underrated by their author when he writes of 'a few crumbs dropped from the literary loaves I distributed in my prime' (CPBS 894).

THEATRICAL CRITICISM

No survey of Shaw's non-dramatic prose, however brief, should ignore the dramatic criticism and the letters. Shaw collected his theatre notices, written for the *Saturday Review*, into three volumes called *Our Theatres in the Nineties*, and one volume of the *Collected Letters* has already appeared, edited by Dan H. Laurence, in addition to the correspondence between Shaw and two famous actresses, Ellen Terry and Mrs. Patrick Campbell, which has been available for some time.

The dramatic criticism is outstanding not only for its wit, but also for the intellectual passion it displays. Shaw could not bear bad art, and his attempts to drive poor plays and what he considered indulgent acting from the stage led him to write in terms which would cause him to be excluded from most theatres today. His criticism of Sir Henry Irving, the greatest actor of his day, was hard-hitting. While admiring Irving's technique, he resented his cavalier way of dealing with the texts of Shakespeare's plays, and we should not overlook the fact that Irving would not produce and act in plays by the new dramatists, including Ibsen— and Shaw! Irving's annoyance with Shaw is scarcely to be wondered at when we read comments such as the following extracts from a notice of Shakespeare's *Richard III*.

> Sir Henry Irving omits these lines, because he plays, as he always does, for a pathetically sublime ending. But we have seen the sublime ending before pretty often.
>
> Once he inadvertently electrified the house by very unexpectedly asking Miss Milton to get further up the stage in the blank verse and penetrating tones of Richard.
>
> She partly had her revenge when she left the stage; for Richard, after playing the scene with her as if he were a Houndsditch salesman cheating a factory girl over a pair of second-hand stockings, naturally could not reach the raptures of the tremendous outburst of elation beginning
>
> > Was ever woman in this humor wooed?
> > Was ever woman in this humor won?
>
> One felt inclined to answer, 'Never, I assure you,' and make an end of the scene there and then.
>
> *Saturday Review* 26 December 1896

Everything Shaw wrote bears the stamp of his personality, and nowhere is this more evident than in his letters. In the introduction to the *Collected Letters 1874–1897*, Dan H. Laurence writes:

> . . . he enormously enjoyed letter writing, and would devote endless hours to it, especially while travelling, carrying huge batches of unanswered correspondence in a sack into which he dipped at any opportunity.

The letters are on a variety of subjects, from finance to literature to politics to love. The reader is referred to the various printed collections. Apart from the eloquence and liveliness that one would expect of Shaw, they are also remarkable for their lack of self-consciousness, as pointed out by Laurence, the editor, when he writes:

> And though Shaw must have been aware even before the turn of the century that his letters were being saved and would one day receive public scrutiny, there is never in them an element of self-consciousness, an awareness that the world is reading them over the author's shoulder.

MUSIC CRITICISM

In Chapter 1 I referred to the wit of Shaw's articles when he was acting as music critic for *The Star* and *The World*. In the Preface to *London Music in 1888–9*, which he wrote in 1935, Shaw disclaimed any worth for the writings of 'Corno di Bassetto', ending, 'Still, you are not compelled to read him. Having read the preface you can shut the book and give it to your worst enemy as a birthday present' (CPBS 867). He is for once being too modest.

Apart from their interest as records of actual performances, the articles on music show how much Shaw did to form popular taste. Largely because of him the later work of Wagner gained a sympathetic audience; Shaw's championing of Wagner's music parallels the case he put up for Ibsen in his dramatic criticism and in *The Quintessence of Ibsenism*. He wrote about music in a comprehensible way, as he despised criticism that dealt only in technicalities. He saw that only professional musicians could understand that kind of criticism 'which was then refined and academic to the point of being unreadable and often nonsensical' (CPBS 866). Penguin Books publish a selection of the music criticism entitled *G.B.S. on Music*, with a foreword by Alec Robertson.

Reading List

BIOGRAPHY

St. John Ervine: *Bernard Shaw* (Constable, 1956).
Blanche Patch: *Thirty Years With G.B.S.* (Gollancz, 1951).
Hesketh Pearson: *Bernard Shaw* (Methuen, 1961. Four Square, 1964).

SHAW'S WORKS

Complete Plays (Odhams Press, no date—Reprinted Paul Hamlyn, 1965).
All the plays are available in *The Standard Edition of the Works of Bernard Shaw* (Constable).
Penguin Books have issued almost all of the major plays in paperback, together with two volumes of one-act plays.
Complete Prefaces (Paul Hamlyn, 1965).
Plays and Players, Essays on the Theatre, selected by A. C. Ward (Oxford, The World's Classics, 1952).
Major Critical Essays (Constable, 1932).
G.B.S. on Music (Penguin Books, 1962).
The Intelligent Woman's Guide to Socialism, Capitalism, Sovietism and Fascism (Penguin Books, 1937).

SHAW'S LETTERS

Collected Letters 1874–1897, edited by Dan H. Laurence (Reinhardt, 1965).
Bernard Shaw and Mrs. Patrick Campbell: Their Correspondence, edited by Alan Dent (Gollancz, 1952).
Ellen Terry and Bernard Shaw: A Correspondence, edited by Christopher St. John (The Fountain Press, New York, and Constable, 1931).

CRITICISM

Eric Bentley: *Bernard Shaw* (New Directions, 1957. Methuen University Paperbacks, 1967).

Harold Fromm: *Bernard Shaw and the Theater in the Nineties* (University of Kansas, 1967).

R. J. Kaufmann (editor): *G. B. Shaw. A Collection of Critical Essays* (Prentice-Hall, 1965).

Fred Mayne: *The Wit and Satire of Bernard Shaw* (Arnold, 1967).

Martin Meisel: *Shaw and the Nineteenth Century Theater* (Princeton, 1963).

Richard M. Ohmann: *Shaw: The Style and The Man* (Wesleyan University Press, 1962).

C. B. Purdom: *A Guide to the Plays of Bernard Shaw* (Methuen, 1963).

J. I. M. Stewart: 'Shaw', in *Eight Modern Writers* (Oxford, 1963).

A. C. Ward: *Bernard Shaw* (Longmans, 1951).

Edmund Wilson: 'Bernard Shaw at Eighty', in *The Triple Thinkers* (Penguin Books, 1962).

SHAW IN THE THEATRE

Thomas C. Kemp: *The Birmingham Repertory Theatre: The Playhouse and the Man* (Cornish Bros. Ltd., Birmingham. Revised edition, 1948).

Raymond Mander and Joe Mitchenson: *Theatrical Companion to Shaw* (Rockliff, 1954).

J. C. Trewin: *The Theatre Since 1900* (Andrew Dakers, 1951).

General Index

Archer, William, 14, 26, 35, 40
Ashmore, Basil, 142
Avenue Theatre, 16, 34

Barker, Harley Granville, 16, 17
Bentley, Eric, 81
Birmingham Repertory Theatre, 17, 64
British Museum, 13, 14, 23
Brophy, Brigid, 117

Campbell, Mrs. Patrick, 138, 154
Candide, 140, 141
Chekhov, Anton, 110, 112, 116
Chocolate Soldier, The, 35
'Corno di Bassetto', 15, 155

Don Giovanni, 44
Down and Out in Paris and London, 67, 68

Evans, Lord Ifor, 93

Fabian Society, 13, 25, 134
Franco, General, 134

G.B.S. on Music, 156
Grein, J. T., 26, 27

Hamlet, 98
Harris, Frank, 15
Hudd, Walter, 133

Ibsen, Henrik, 14, 16, 19, 154
Independent Theatre, 26, 27
Irving, Sir Henry, 16, 154

Jackson, Sir Barry, 17, 18

Laurence, Dan H., 154, 155
Lawrence, T. E., 133
Lee, George John Vandaleur, 12
Limbert, Roy, 18
Luigi Pirandello, 1867–1936, 121

MacKechnie, Donald, 61
Malvern Festival, 17, 18, 134
Mander, Raymond, 21
Mansfield, Richard, 40, 42
Marx, Karl, 13
Mitchenson, Joe, 21
Mozart, W. A., 44

Murray, Alma, 34
Murray, Gilbert, 134
Mussolini, Benito, 134, 135, 136

National Theatre, 61, 62
Nietzsche, Friedrich, 57, 134

Ohmann, Richard M., 149
Orwell, George, 67, 68
Osborne, John, 27, 101, 146

Pall Mall Gazette, The, 14
Patch, Blanche, 10, 133, 143
Pearson, Hesketh, 19, 143, 149, 153

Royal Academy of Dramatic Art, 16
Royal Court Theatre, 17, 27

Saturday Review, 15, 154
Shakespeare, William, 18, 19, 113, 122, 132, 145, 148, 154
Shaw, Mrs. Bernard (Charlotte), 17, 138
Shaw, George Carr, 11
Shaw, Mrs. George Carr, 11–12
Shaw: The Style and the Man, 149
Short History of English Literature, A, 93
Stanislavsky, Konstantin, 122
Starkie, Walter, 121
Strauss, Oscar, 35
Sweet, Henry, 134

Terry, Ellen, 138, 154
Theatrical Companion to Shaw, 21
Thirty Years With G.B.S., 133, 143
Thorndike, Sybil, 88
Trebitsch, Siegfried, 23
Triple Thinkers, The, 119

Vedrenne, J. E., 17
Voltaire, 140, 141

Wagner, Richard, 45, 155
Walkley, A. B., 44
Webb, Beatrice, 13, 29
Webb, Sidney, 13, 29, 134
Wells, H. G., 13, 29, 132
Wilde, Oscar, 28, 68
Williams, Clifford, 61
Wilson, Edmund, 119
World, The, 14, 15, 40, 155

Index to Shaw's Works

Main entries are indicated in heavy type

Androcles and the Lion, 23, 66, 72, **82–87,**
  88, 120, 143, 149, 150, 152
Annajanska, 140
Apple Cart, The, 17, 18, 20, 57, 119,
  124, 130, 131, 132, 136, 137, 138
Arms and the Man, 15, 16, 19, 34,
  35–40, 41, 134, 146
Augustus Does His Bit, 119, 129

Back to Methuselah, 17, 19, 20, 43, 52,
  60–63, 137, 141–142, 149, 150, 152,
  153
Black Girl in Search of God, The, **140–**
  142
Buoyant Billions, 18

Caesar and Cleopatra, 20, 91, **97–102,**
  119
Candida, 34, **40–42**
Captain Brassbound's Conversion, 50

Devil's Disciple, The, 19, 147, 148
Doctor's Dilemma, The, 16, 20, **102–109,**
  119, 122, 149
'*Don Juan in Hell*', 44–45, **50–58,** 60–
  61, 63, 121

Everybody's Political What's What, 139,
  140

Farfetched Fables, 153

Geneva, 131, **134–136**
Getting Married, 152

Heartbreak House, 18, 57, **109–119,** 131,
  152

In Good King Charles's Golden Days, 18,
  97, 120, 122, 137, 138
*Intelligent Woman's Guide to Socialism,
  Capitalism, Sovietism and Fascism,
  The*, 18, 139

Jitta's Atonement, 23

London Music in 1888–9, 11–12, 155

Major Barbara, 17, 20, 66, **67–82,** 87, 88,
  122, 124, 134, 142, 151
Man and Superman, 13, 17, 19, 43, **44–**
  60, 63, 65, 120, 121, 124
Man of Destiny, The, 91, 98, 146
Millionairess, The, 25, 93, 136, 137
Misalliance, 90, 112, 115, 116, 136
Mrs. Warren's Profession, 19, 26, 27, 28,
  29–33, 34, 41, 43, 67, 119, 122, 142,
  144, 145–146

O'Flaherty, V.C., 119, 129–130
On the Rocks, 121, 149
Our Theatres in the Nineties, 154

Philanderer, The, 27, 28, 33
Plays Pleasant, 33, 34, 40, 42, 144, 146,
  147
Plays Unpleasant, 25, 33, 42, 144, 147,
  148
Prefaces, The, **142–153**
Press Cuttings, 130, 134
Pygmalion, 20, 23, 25, 33, **93–96,** 97,
  102, 119, 124, 128–129, 134

Quintessence of Ibsenism, The, 155

Saint Joan, 17, 20, 53, 66, **87–92,** 98,
  102, 131, 145, 149, 150–151, 152, 153
Simpleton of the Unexpected Isles, The,
  18, 20, 43, **63–64,** 120, 121
Sixteen Self Sketches, 10

Three Plays for Puritans, 144, 147, 148
Too True to be Good, 18, 131, **132–133**

Village Wooing, 122, 131–132

Widowers' Houses, 14, 15, 26, 28, 32,
  33, 34, 35, 67, 94, 119, 124, 144
Why She Would Not, 23

You Never Can Tell, 34, 65, **124–129,**
  146, 147